Jody D. Woodworth, Ph.D.

Perspectives of Strategic Planning in Higher Education

A Grounded Theory Qualitative Study

LAP LAMBERT Academic Publishing

Impressum/Imprint (nur für Deutschland/only for Germany)
Bibliografische Information der Deutschen Nationalbibliothek: Die Deutsche Nationalbibliothek verzeichnet diese Publikation in der Deutschen Nationalbibliografie; detaillierte bibliografische Daten sind im Internet über http://dnb.d-nb.de abrufbar.
Alle in diesem Buch genannten Marken und Produktnamen unterliegen warenzeichen-, marken- oder patentrechtlichem Schutz bzw. sind Warenzeichen oder eingetragene Warenzeichen der jeweiligen Inhaber. Die Wiedergabe von Marken, Produktnamen, Gebrauchsnamen, Handelsnamen, Warenbezeichnungen u.s.w. in diesem Werk berechtigt auch ohne besondere Kennzeichnung nicht zu der Annahme, dass solche Namen im Sinne der Warenzeichen- und Markenschutzgesetzgebung als frei zu betrachten wären und daher von jedermann benutzt werden dürften.

Coverbild: www.ingimage.com

Verlag: LAP LAMBERT Academic Publishing GmbH & Co. KG
Dudweiler Landstr. 99, 66123 Saarbrücken, Deutschland
Telefon +49 681 3720-310, Telefax +49 681 3720-3109
Email: info@lap-publishing.com

Approved by: Lincoln, University of Nebraska, Diss, 2009

Herstellung in Deutschland:
Schaltungsdienst Lange o.H.G., Berlin
Books on Demand GmbH, Norderstedt
Reha GmbH, Saarbrücken
Amazon Distribution GmbH, Leipzig
ISBN: 978-3-8465-0441-3

Imprint (only for USA, GB)
Bibliographic information published by the Deutsche Nationalbibliothek: The Deutsche Nationalbibliothek lists this publication in the Deutsche Nationalbibliografie; detailed bibliographic data are available in the Internet at http://dnb.d-nb.de.
Any brand names and product names mentioned in this book are subject to trademark, brand or patent protection and are trademarks or registered trademarks of their respective holders. The use of brand names, product names, common names, trade names, product descriptions etc. even without a particular marking in this works is in no way to be construed to mean that such names may be regarded as unrestricted in respect of trademark and brand protection legislation and could thus be used by anyone.

Cover image: www.ingimage.com

Publisher: LAP LAMBERT Academic Publishing GmbH & Co. KG
Dudweiler Landstr. 99, 66123 Saarbrücken, Germany
Phone +49 681 3720-310, Fax +49 681 3720-3109
Email: info@lap-publishing.com

Printed in the U.S.A.
Printed in the U.K. by (see last page)
ISBN: 978-3-8465-0441-3

1

TABLE OF CONTENTS

Abstract 6

Chapter 1—Introduction 7

    Statement of the Problem... 8

    Purpose of the Study 8

    Research Questions.. 9

    Definition of Terms... 9

Chapter 2—Literature Review... 11

    Historical Perspective 11

    Strategic Planning in Academia.. 11

    Accreditation as Driving Forces for Strategic Planning 15

    Models for Strategic Planning 17

    Qualitative Approaches to Strategic Planning 21

Chapter 3—Methodology 25

    Assumptions & Rationale for Qualitative Methodology 25

    Participants.. 26

    Creation of Interview Questions 29

    Contacting the Participants 29

    Data Collection 30

    Validity and Reliability... 31

    Data Analysis.. 32

    Ethical Considerations 34

    Summary of Methodology 34

2

Chapter 4—Demographics 37

    Demographics & Participant Characteristics 37

    Summary of Demographics 37

    Participant Educational & Experiential Preparation 41

    Summary of Participant Educational & Experiential Preparation 46

Chapter 5—Grounded Theory Storyline 48

    Section I: Accountability & Transparency 48

        External Driving Forces 49

        Internal Driving Forces 53

        Participation & Publication 55

        Limitations & Enhancements of Participation 57

        Summary of Section I Accountability & Transparency 60

    Section II: Process & Framework of a Strategic Plan 63

        Creation Process of Strategic Planning 63

        Facilitator Discussion 64

        Framework for the Model Creation 69

        Essential Elements of Strategic Plans 71

        Review and Implementation of Strategic Plans 76

        Limitation & Enhancements of Essential Elements 77

        Summary of Section II Process & Framework 80

    Section III: Achievement of Successful Strategic Plans 86

        Measurement Tools 87

        Student Learning Outcomes Assessment 87

3

Operational Objectives 91

Summary of Section III Achievement of Successful Plans 93

Section IV: Budget Integration & Resource Allocation 94

Summary of Section IV: Budget Integration 97

Chapter 6—Results of Research Questions 98

Research Question 1 98

Research Question 2 98

Research Question 3 99

Research Question 4 99

Research Question 5 101

Research Question 6 101

Chapter 7—Grounded Theory 102

Grounded Theory & Model 102

Theory I: Driving Forces 103

Theory II: Communication & Education 106

Theory III: Assessment Integration 106

Theory IV: Assessment & Budget Allocation 107

Chapter 8—Recommendations 109

Implications for Practice 109

Implications for Research 110

References 111

4

LIST OF TABLES

Table 1   Description of Institution Types by IACBE 28

Table 2   Demographics and Participant Characteristics 38

Table 3a   Participant Educational Preparation... 42

Table 3b   Participant Experiential Preparation 43

5

LIST OF FIGURES

Figure 1   IACBE Integrated Strategic Planning Model 20

Figure 2   Simplified Strategic Planning Model in Business & Academics.................................... 24

Figure 3   Driving Forces to Strategic Plan 62

Figure 4   Top-Down Differences to Literature 84

Figure 5   Bottom-Up Differences to Literature... 85

Figure 6   Grounded Theory Model – Driving Forces 104

Figure 7   Grounded Theory Model - Strategic Planning... 105

6

ABSTRACT

This dissertation examined the perspectives of higher education business unit leaders on the creation and implementation of a strategic plan. The purpose of this qualitative study was to reveal the perspectives of leaders in academic business units/divisions regarding their ability to create and implement effective strategic plans. These individuals, who have been exposed in either their educational or experiential background to the models and practices of strategic planning, should be the expert in pulling together working strategic plans for their institutions.

The data were collected from the higher education business unit leaders focusing on open ended questions in five topical areas: (1) education/experience, (2) accountability and transparency, (3) process and framework, (4) achievement of successful plans, and (5) budget integration. The researcher addressed limitations and challenges in each area. This research explored evidence of actual use of models found in literature, the extent to which they are used, and evidence of the successful implementation by leaders.

Four emergent themes emergent themes were the basis of four grounded theories for a strategic plan model in academia. Implications for business leaders were recommended for the future research.

The emergent themes analyzed from the participant's responses of this study addressed 1) accountability and transparency, which included driving forces to strategic plan, 2) the process and framework of their plan creation, 3) Achievement of successful plans, and 4) budget integration and resource allocation. The grounded theories created from this study were created from analysis of the emergent themes.

7

CHAPTER 1
INTRODUCTION

Strategic Planning, used historically in military operations for the deployment of human and capital resources, has been used in various forms by corporate America since the 1950s. By the mid-1960s and throughout the 1970s, strategic planning was implemented in most large corporations. Even the federal government used a Planning-Programming-Budgeting System (PPBS) during this time. The use of strategic planning models in Corporate America did not yield the hoped for return on investments and business returned to the status quo. A revival of these models occurred in the 1990s; business, healthcare, education, and other industries are still practicing some form of strategic planning today. The term *strategic management* is used at many colleges and universities as the subtitle for the capstone course in business administration and business policy that integrates material from all business courses (David, 2007).

The process of adapting business models to academic culture has caused friction in higher education. Issues that plague higher education include the complex structure of colleges and universities based on traditions and individual silos of expertise and the failure to adapt to new environmental demands while assessing internal achievement; the latter makes it difficult to pull together a formalized strategic plan. Institutional leaders are required to analyze their strengths and weaknesses internally. Infrastructure issues that hinder growth and inefficiency within the institution lead to the loss of competitive advantage. Strategic planning is "a disciplined effort to produce fundamental decisions and actions that shape and guide what an organization is, what it does, and why it does it" (Bryson, 1996, p.53).

External opportunities and the focus of growth generate the need for a more efficient infrastructure in organizations. Planning for this effort has resulted in a variety of strategic planning models created from decades of research. Academic leadership is required to adapt practices of strategic management principles from corporate industries and overcome the traditional challenges of higher education.

Statement of the Problem

Higher education is crucial to our society and must change to address the challenges in higher education. In this consumer-driven environment, students increasingly care little about the distinctions that sometimes preoccupy the academic establishment . . . instead, they care about results (Spellings,

2006). Higher education institutions can no longer operate with internal silos; they must direct movement toward concepts of efficiency and accountability. Higher education has a duty of accountability to the public, governmental and private sources of funding. Academic leaders must rise to the challenge of the new century.

Purpose of the Study

The purpose of this qualitative study was to reveal the perspectives of higher education business unit leaders about the creation and implementation of a strategic plan. These individuals, who have been exposed in either their educational or experiential background to the models and practices of strategic planning, should be experts in pulling together working strategic plans for their units.

Business unit leaders have their own perspectives of creation and implementation of strategic models and formats that are often the modification of past models and development of new models. Because there is complexity in higher education institutional structures, there is little room for new processes, creation of previously established elements, and other modifications in strategic planning models. Are these leaders, through education or experience, prepared to create strategic plans? Is there a possibility that these leaders use specific strategic planning models for higher education, or are the models modified to fit the leader's or institution's needs? If these models are modified, emerging themes can be use to develop plausible relationships among concepts, sets of concepts, processes and limitations of creating and implementing a strategic plan.

First the historical concept of strategic planning through studies in both business and educational research was explored. Second, identification of strategic planning models, both historical and evolving, were used for comparison to study results.

The established qualitative research method of grounded theory, which was introduced by Glaser & Strauss in 1967, was employed in this inquiry. According to Byrne (2001), grounded theory provides the researcher with strategies that can be used to build theories in areas previously unexplored or under explored.

The researcher was the main source of data collection. Merriam (1998) asserted that qualitative research primarily employs an inductive research strategy, which builds abstractions, concepts, hypotheses, or theories rather than testing existing theories. This research explored the literature based models found in literature and, the extent to which they were used, and evidence of the success when implemented by leaders. The researcher, through emergent themes, developed a grounded theory and model for academic strategic planning as perceived by the business unit leaders.

Research Questions

Creswell (2009) stated, "In grounded theory, the questions may be directed toward generating a theory of some process" (p.129). The perspectives of higher education business unit leaders were obtained to create a picture of reality for the creation and implementation of strategic plans.

1. How has the business leader's education prepared them for strategic planning?
2. What drives the need for strategic planning in the institution and business units?
3. How are their strategic plans implemented in their programs and integrated within their college/university?
4. How are their strategic plans created?
5. What are the constraints/limitations of the strategic planning process?
6. What changes in their current process would produce a more successful product?

Definition of Terms

For the purpose of this study, the following terms have been identified to give the reader a clear understanding of the topic.

Business Unit: Higher education institutions have various areas designated for business education and are named various titles school, department, or division of business. For this study the term business unit is used to identify the area designated for business education.

Business Program Leader: The leaders may hold various titles such as Chair, Director, Dean, Assistant Dean, which may be used interchangeably. Higher education institutions have various titles for the person with direct leadership and accountability for the business unit, school, or division of business. Leaders are responsible for the curriculum, student learning outcomes and strategic planning for the business unit.

Higher Learning Commission (HLC): The HLC coordinates accreditation activity in the United States for six *regional* agencies providing institutional accreditation on a geographical basis – Middle States, New England, North Central, Northwest, Southern, and Western.

Market Analysis: Sometimes called environmental scanning, it is data gathered to track industry competitive trends, emerging market opportunities, governmental and even the positioning of the organization demographically.

Program Strategies: Means by which long-term objectives will be achieved. These may include program development, growth, expansion or building.

Program Objectives: Short-term milestones to be measureable and achievable to reach long-term objectives. Examples would be both operational and learning assessment annually.

Outcomes Assessment: Student learning outcomes is a set of measurement tools for student learning identified by the department or institution.

Regional Accreditation: A regionally accredited U.S. based college or university that is granting undergraduate and/or graduate degrees.

STEP Analysis: A tool to identify external Social, Technical, Economical and Political competitive environments as they relate to the institution.

Strategic Planning: The process of determining a unit's long-term goals and subsequent identification the best approach for achieving those goals.

SWOT Analysis: A tool that identifies internal Strengths, Weakness, and internal Opportunity and Threats to the institution/unit.

CHAPTER 2
LITERATURE REVIEW

This literature review provides an historical backdrop for strategic planning within the business industry and documents the attempts to integrate the strategic planning models into higher education institutions.

Historical Perspective

A pioneer of strategic planning, Mintzberg (1978), defined planning as a formalized procedure to produce an articulated result in the form of an integrated system of decisions, with emphasis on process before product. Business industry's strategic planning model relies on immediate financial results. These financial results are based on projections, future sales, market environment, and common elements that drive long range strategic planning. Strategic planning, then, stresses the importance of making decisions that ensure the organization's ability to respond successfully to changes in the environment (Pacios, 2004).

Strategic planning has evolved through the decades. Cyert & March (1963) claimed that strategy is a goal or precedent in an institution; Mintzberg (1978) defined strategic plans and claimed that strategic planning could represent a pattern, position, and perspective. Strategists like Porter (1980, 1985) tried to capture more unique aspects of the firm's internal strategic behavior. The theorists agree that attention should be given to institutional content review, action plans, and implementation of the plans. Current plans reflect a strategic planning process consisting of three stages: strategy formulation, strategy implementation, and strategy evaluation (David, 2007). Few theorists question the function of strategic planning as a guide to the achievement of a vision, goals and objectives created by the institution. However, the development of strategic planning has produced in-depth, detailed, and cumbersome documents that are rarely flexible in a changing environment.

Strategic Planning in Academia

One of the first strategic planning documents in academia focused on key elements of planning. The landmark works of George Keller (1993) produced distinguishing characteristics of the strategic process in higher education (pp. 143-152):

- An institution is active and not passive

12

- An institution takes into consideration the external environment
- The strategy operates in a sensitive and competitive market
- Strategic planning concentrates on decisions and is oriented to action.
- Strategic planning is a blend of quantitative and qualitative factors and is participatory and controversial
- The success of the institution is the focus.

This process was used by academic leadership until Basham & Lunenburg (1989) asserted that strategic planning concepts are not well-defined; they asserted that, although there exists a number of definitions pertaining to educational strategic planning; there was a specific lack of uniform, discrete definitions of educational strategic planning models. Exploration in the use and implement strategic planning has continued in higher education as institutions provide diverse programs to an ever changing population.

To the extent that planning was relevant to higher education, it generally was about expansion and new facilities, which eventually led to the creation of the Society of College and University Planning (SCUP) formed in 1996 with a primary interest in campus/facilities planning (Dooris, 2003).

Educational institutions, like other service organizations, have realized the importance of differentiation in their programs, delivery systems, and prospective students. The knowledge-based economy in which the institutions operate emphasized interest in more diverse programs in higher learning, in response to job requirements. The department or administrative units involved in strategic planning are required to identify and establish these unique programs within the larger university community. The challenges are (a) competition for scarce resources and (b) the ability to strategically carry out their individual action plans. This pressure can be observed in multiple units of colleges and universities. Much like the departments of corporate America, they must become efficient and effective. Competition is perceived to be needed to obtain qualified students and resources and provide quality programs with internal support for those activities. Greater decreases in federal funding, increasing demands for student services, aid, faculty services, technology, and learning outcomes escalate the pressures to manage all of these factors and fall on the institutional leadership (Edge, 2004).

The accountability of an institution should provide evidence of compliance to their mission and goals both in operations and measurement of student learning outcomes. Such assessments should be consistent with the strategies and action plans of an institution. The plan should outline a detailed, multi-year plan with action items to be accomplished (Bryson, 1996). Others maintain that strategic planning provides a framework for action that is embedded in the mind set of the organization and its employees. It is a process by which guiding members of an organization envision its future and develop the necessary procedures and operations to achieve that future (Goodstein, Nolan, & Pfeiffer, 1993).

Assumptions could also be made that there is some form of strategic planning in most institutions of higher education, yet Keller (1993) acknowledged that a considerable number of initial efforts had failed to produce strategic changes. It is estimated that for every three institutions that had initiated a planning process in the 1980s, two had abandoned and had gone back to "business as usual" (Jones, 1990). In 1994, the American Council on Education (ACE) examined the state of strategic planning on eight campuses. Using the previous studies by Keller, ACE found mixed strategic planning efforts and some failures. Cutright (1999) asserted that colleges too easily assume that society's evolution is reasonably orderly, predictable and tidily sequential.

Past attempts to connect strategic planning with higher education institutions have encountered differences in governance, structure, language, values, analytical demands, exceptions, spans of control, and decision-making. These differences have contributed to an unhappy marriage between higher education and strategic planning (Dolence, 2004). Despite these differences, the majority of institutional plans are driven by the need for new student enrollment and acquisition of funds to remain viable.

Change in governance, accountability, assessment, performance measurement and quality reviews are likely to continue to find acceptance within higher education. . . change management and leading change in the private sector are ultimately comparable to strategic planning in higher education (Spencer, 2005). Kotter (1995) defined fundamental changes of how business is conducted in order to help cope with new, more challenging market environments. Kotter's eight steps for understanding change included strategic planning and the creation of short-term wins in order to show progress and build confidence in institutions.

Colleges and universities use various strategic planning paradigms resulting in a broad range of measured successes. Institutions have processes in place for budgets, strategies, and learning outcomes assessment but rarely integrate them in unified form. This lack of integration often leads to frustration throughout the organizations and stakeholders. More importantly, it may also result in suboptimal performance (Roller et al., 2004). There is no literature to help a campus understand whether it should engage in a reengineering of campus governance and planning process and what some of the possible consequences might be for doing so (Kezar, 2005).

In addition to the formulation and integration of strategy, the environment is changing. David (2007) identified population shifts from the Northeast and Midwest to the Southeast and West as another factor causing trauma for educational institutions that have not planned for changing enrollments.

Boundaries of competition are also blurred through the implementation of online courses and degree programs. Interactive computer networks, course delivery platforms, and telecommunications have changed the face of education. Not only is the cost of resources increasing, it is absolutely necessary to have online capabilities to stay competitive in the academic industry. Developing and implementing strategy, an important element of success in a changing environment, allows for strategic actions to emerge when the environmental conditions require strategic flexibility (Hitt et al., 2007).

Dolence (2004) offered an approach to strategic planning for higher education institutions based on the learner. Traditionally, monitoring institutional performance has been on the basis of internal and external environmental scanning. A SWOT analysis is one of the basic, straightforward tools that provides direction and serves as a basis for the development of strategic plans. It accomplishes this by assessing an organizations strengths (what an organization can do) and weaknesses (what an organization cannot do) in addition to opportunities (potential favorable conditions for an organization) and threats (potential unfavorable conditions for an organization). SWOT analysis is an important step in planning and its value is often underestimated despite the simplicity in creation. The role of SWOT analysis is to take the information from the environmental analysis and separate it into internal issues (strengths and weaknesses) and external issues (opportunities and threats). Once this is completed, SWOT analysis determines if the information indicates something that will assist the firm in accomplishing its objectives (a strength or opportunity), or if it indicates an obstacle that must be overcome or minimized to achieve desired results (weakness or threat) (Ferrell, 1998).

Another tool of measurement is the learner outcomes approach is centered on the curriculum; measureable student learning objectives and the creation of strategies and formulation of action plans are focused on how learning occurs and how the learner is affected. The regional accrediting bodies for higher education quality have seen the need for institutions to develop long range plans to accomplish their overall mission and goals. In addition, educational leaders use strategic planning to allow the organization to achieve its vision. Bryson (1995,) asserted that leaders must be masterful in this process to allow the organization to "...fulfill [its] mission, meet [its] mandates, and satisfy [its] constituents in the years ahead" (p. 41).

Birnbaum's (2000) study of academic leadership asked interviewees to name important leaders in their campuses. Forty-four percent of the respondents named the dean. In large, decentralized universities, deans were mentioned more frequently than anyone else, including the president. Purpose, vision and value- directed leadership have been consistent ideas that surface in the study of leadership (Martin, 1993). Organizational leaders should be masters of understanding and directing the vision of an institution that embodies the cultural beliefs, values and assumptions of its members (Schein, 1985).

Accreditation as Driving Forces for Strategic Planning

As previously stated in the introduction, higher education is crucial to our society and must change to address the challenges to higher education. In this consumer-driven environment, students increasingly care little about the distinctions that sometimes preoccupy the academic establishment...instead; they care about results (Spellings, 2006). Higher education institutions can no longer operate with internal silos; it must direct movement toward concepts of efficiency and accountability. Higher education has a duty of accountability to the public, governmental and private sources of funding; academic leaders must rise to the challenge of the new century.

Urgent reform needs were outlined by the Spellings Commission (2006). Findings by the Commission resulted in six broad recommendations (Ruben et al., 2008):

1. Student academic preparation should be improved and financial aid made available so that more students are able to access and afford a quality higher education.
2. The entire student financial aid system should be simplified restructured and provided with incentives to better manage costs and measure performance.
3. A "robust culture of accountability and transparency" should be cultivated throughout the higher education system, aided by new systems of data measurement and a publicly available information database with comparable college information. There should also be a greater focus on student learning and development of a more outcome-focused accreditation system.
4. Colleges and universities should embrace continuous innovation and quality improvement.

5. Federal investments should be targeted to areas critical to America's global competitiveness, such as math, science, and foreign languages.

6. A strategy for lifelong learning should be developed to increase awareness and understanding of the importance of a college education to every American's future.

A major controversial recommendation is that of accountability and transparency of the higher education system and improvement of measurements. This controversy emphasized the increased roles and responsibilities of the accrediting bodies. There is a greater need for leaders to articulate the need for identifying new initiatives and challenges and to seek new opportunities for collaborations (p. 20). All institutions in the U.S. are expected to be subject to scrutiny. For those institutions that choose to embrace changes – and even those who do not – there is likely to come a time of accountability. Those institutions that begin strategic planning to incorporate and measure outcomes, and address changes in higher education, will be ahead of the game.

The Spellings Commission review emphasized that there may be a substantial increase in the roles and responsibilities of the regional accrediting bodies. During the review of the Spellings Commission, the Council on Higher Education Accreditation (CHEA) and programmatic and regional accreditation associations brought renewed reflection to the process of reviewing and improving the accreditation process including the issues of assessment, transparency, and improvements within the standards and documentation (Ruben et al., 2008). CHEA and the Higher Learning Commission (HLC) coordinate accreditation activity in the United States for six regional agencies that provide institutional accreditation on a geographical basis – Middle States, New England, North Central, Northwest, Southern, and Western (*Handbook of Accreditation Standards*, 2003). These institution-level accrediting bodies deal with specifics such as the accreditation of particular disciplines and Web-based learning.

Accreditation's 1998 Recognition Standards defined an expectation for evidence of policies and procedures that stress planning and implementing strategies for change (Dooris, 2003). Accreditation is a "gold standard" in higher education, and transfer credits and federal funding are key factors for those institutions that choose to be accredited based on standards set forth by the regional bodies. These factors can be the catalyst for most institutions to create, implement and measure strategic plans.

In addition, specialty accrediting bodies, such as the IACBE for business, can require an institution to be regionally accredited prior to consideration for specialty accreditation. Requirements of student learning outcomes and strategic planning are part of the expectations of the specialty accreditation in business.

Another possible catalyst to the implementation of strategic plans in institutions is the alignment of the Malcolm Baldridge Award for Performance Excellence in Education. The Malcolm Baldridge criteria create a framework through which an institution can demonstrate its success and efficiency, affirming the quality of the institution in the academic industry; these criteria were historically grounded in business industries. The Educational Criteria for Performance Excellence validates an academic organization's management practices and performance excellence in higher education and helps to create a competitive edge to acquire students (source Ford, 2000)

The Malcolm Baldrige National Quality Award allows the organization to gain recognition and respect in higher education as organizations compete for students in the global marketplace. The Malcolm Baldrige Criteria for Performance Excellence (CPE) are designed to help organizations enhance competitiveness through the delivery of value to customers and improvements of overall organizational performance and capabilities. There are seven categories in the award criteria, and the development of strategy requires consideration of the following: 1) environment/market, 2) customer, 3) financial and societal risk, 4) human resource capabilities, 5) company operational capabilities, and 6) supplier/partnership capabilities (Ford, 2000).

Although theorists have discussed the validity of the CPE award criteria, there is little scholarly literature examining the effectiveness of strategic planning. These theorists question the formality and comprehensiveness of a plan. Most, however, agree that elements outside of their control such as environmental competition, technological innovation, and new emergent markets (Mintzberg, 1978) are best recognized and solved through a strategic planning process. Modern researchers continue to acknowledge that the uncertainty, complexity, and conflict that characterized the difficulty of strategic problems constituted a possible source for profitability (Ford, 2000).

Models for Strategic Planning

Several research models and publications are acknowledged by leading researchers who suggest a comprehensive process for the creation and implementation of higher education strategic plans for public and nonprofit institutions (Bryson & Alston, 1996). Some strategic planning models have a process similar to the business industry with scanning analysis, identifying stakeholders; and formulating strategies and effective implementation and evaluation. Birnbaum, (2000) focused in particular on higher education's adoption of management "fads" in which he included strategic planning and total quality management (Dooris, 2003).

One of the first investigations using practical experiences of strategic planning leaders involved the Total Quality Management (TQM) process in business. A grounded theory approach was used in 2001 by Leonard and McAdam linking organizational behavior to explore general phenomena of TQM based on practical experience. This was done through semi-structured interviews in which key categories emerged as significant elements of the relationship between TQM and corporate strategy. In early 1991, TQM emerged as a tactical tool for developing corporate strategy and to achieve goals successfully. The relationship between (TQM) and strategic planning was seen as a key competitive factor; however, quality was allowed to become an incidental and secondary factor, if considered at all in the formulation of a competitive strategy (Leonard & McAdam, 2001).

Innovative colleges and universities share high quality processes and business practices with other institutions in order to promote best practice. Benchmarking, described as a continuous, systematic process for evaluating the products, services, and work processes of organizations, is recognized as representing best practices for the purposes of organization improvement and is an extension of the TQM process (Spendolini, 1992). Colleges should understand that what works at some industries may not work in higher education organizations and that extraordinary procedures at a Quaker college or big state university in a farm state may not work at a Baptist college or private urban university. One method of benchmarking is to tag those operations that are reported to be done with exceptional excellence at other colleges or universities (Stralser, 1997).

If an institution chooses to provide evidence of success in achieving their mission and goals, what other factors drive an institution to plan strategically? As stated previously in the literature review, regional accreditation agencies encourage the management of key indicators to validate the efficient use of public and private funding in education, that is to operate efficiently and with accountability (McLaughlin et al., 2005). This holistic approach requires an institution to decide how to measure progress, collect appropriate data, analyze data, compile and create understandable action plans.

Developing accountability in operations that affect student enrollment and that contribute to the high cost of higher education is done through key performance indicators (KPI) (McLaughlin et al., 2005). These indicators measure the success of institutional operations and strategic, data-driven decisions support enables a manager to evaluate the benefit of dollars spent on both instructional activities (learning outcomes) and non-classroom activities (operations), tangible and intangible. At California State University, Los Angeles, administration found that the KPI was not effective for their institution due to an over-emphasis on data collection and a neglect of broader planning issues. What was needed was a planning process that was driven by "higher level" analysis and broader understanding of the links between mission, strategy, and organizational direction (Cordeiro, 2002). The institutional evaluation of their strategic planning process focused on developing a plan to strategically guide its future however, they found that even though the planning contributed to the success of the organization, it did not eliminate political, management or administrative issues or change the organizational culture, values, and behavior (p. 31).

Kaplan and Norton's introduction of the balanced scorecard tool of accountability into the business arena has been recently used for educational institutions. This evaluation tool gives administration a more balanced approach to the financial, business processes, and growth of an institution. A portfolio is created to capture the processes and areas of the institution's key functions. These indicators can show trends over time and external comparisons to other institutions can also be made. The challenge is to get the numerous divisions and departments throughout the college/university to buy-in to the need for data-driven processes and to use the resources made available to them (McLaughlin et al., 2005).

Scenario planning, introduced in 2004 by Chermack, was a method of planning used to evaluate performance-based institutions in terms of economic, systems, and psychological domains at the individual group and organizational levels. The quantitative research of Chermack was another method of strategy-making that explored the psychological performance (learning) at the organizational level. The research constructed dimensions of learning in the organization. Questions were directed at individual behaviors, ultimately creating strategy related to human resources. This scenario planning is the vehicle that links the work of Human Resource professionals to the strategic context of organizations (Chermack et al., 2006).

Research provides evidence of several reasons why there is a desire to plan, how plans evolve, and how they are accomplished and monitored. A study published in 2000 by Schwarz used the grounded theory approach to study the development of strategic ideas in a single, multinational organization. The author stated that grounded theory has rarely been used to research strategic decision process. He found that the use of this research method was particularly appropriate in developing a

20

theoretical framework. Thus, it is suggested that grounded theory would be particularly useful for strategic ideas development where previous knowledge of the subject is limited (Schwarz, 2002).

A more focused area of business education (Roller et al., 2004) also offered an integrated strategic planning model for departments of business in higher education. The model delineated the elements of (a)environmental scanning, (b) strategy formulation, and (c) implementation evaluation and control. The emergent model offered by the IACBE to its members is shown in Figure 1. This mode depicts the integration of business unit and in most institutions (and business schools), there is little integration of strategic planning, budgeting, and outcomes assessment In most cases, there are separate plans that are generated by poorly-integrated processes (Roller et al., 2004).

This integration of strategic planning with the overall institutional strategic plan is known as a "bottom-up" approach to strategic planning. This "grass roots" or "bottom-up" approach to strategic planning has been accomplished with input from a variety of organizational constituents or stakeholders, as opposed to the traditional "top-down" planning typically employed and directed by

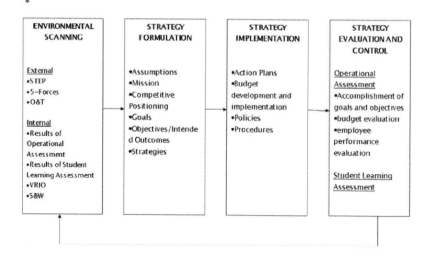

Roller et al, 2004

Figure 1. IACBE integrated strategic planning model.

21

central office administrators (Rieger, 1994). Rieger also suggest that this integration is likely to occur on an incremental basis at most institutions and will be significantly influenced by the culture of the institution. Henri Fayol, also known as the founding father of the administration school ... first to describe management as a top-down process based on planning and the organization of people. He described a good plan of action by administration should be flexible, continuous, relevant and accurate, as it unifies the organization by focusing on the nature, priorities and condition of the business, longer-term predictions for the industry and economy, the intuitions of key thinkers, and strategic sector analyses from specialist staff groups (Fayol, 1975).

The bottom-up versus top-down approaches is clarified in Roller et al. (2004) and is important to this research topic. The top-down approach to planning is initiated by institutional administration that establishes the mission, goals and objectives. Every unit with budget responsibilities in the institution uses the initial plan and creates and implements a strategic plan for the unit. An important element of this type of approach is that the budget is set and may act as a limitation to the plan.

The bottom-up model requires the individual units to initiate and create a strategic plan based on the mission and goals of the institution. The unit plans include recommendations for budgets based on their ability to carry out the objectives and actions of the unit. This plan is then compiled for each area; the administration then decides upon the priority of objectives for each area; the budget can then be negotiated and is reflective of the priorities. Items that do not get funded for the academic year can be placed in the long-range plans or alternative grants and funding can specifically target those needs. An issue of the plan is that it may remain in the hands of the individual budget centers and never be integrated with other areas of the institution (Roller et al., 2000).

Qualitative Approaches to Strategic Planning

The literature, to this point, has provided tools and evidence of a tool's validity, both in business and in education. The research is based predominately on a deductive process in which a more scientific approach to formulation of theories from large data samples is used to demonstrate validity. Empirical data suggests gaps in educational strategic planning (Hambright & Diamantes, 2004b). Literature is replete with educational strategic planning models; however, these models are prescriptive in their nature; fewer than half of the reviewed educational strategic planning models contained field examples (Bryson, 1995).

An assumption can also be made that faculty and administration in units/divisions of business education within institutions of higher education should have familiarity and expertise in conducting strategic planning process as the majority of research has been conducted by these individuals (Martin, 1993). The grounded theory research by Martin explored the analysis of effective academic leadership at research universities. Through open-ended interviews the author found that deans regarded planning to be a prominent part of the communication systems and leadership style of their positions. Planning appeared to function as a means of communication with faculty and other areas of the institution. Although some deans used plans to work toward achieving agreed upon goals of their areas, written plans were often shelved and rarely reviewed or used for directional purposes. About one half of the deans interviewed did not use the planning process as an integral part of their leadership.

As the former executive editor of Planning for Higher Education stated, "There is no one way to do university planning" (Keller,1999). What might have worked in the 1980s may not be as effective in a more current knowledge-based society. His recognition of the initial six characteristics cited in 1983 for academic strategic plans has been modified to four distinct types of higher educational institutions and a realization that plans must also change. The new higher education configuration is paraphrased from the 1999 article by Keller, *The Emerging Third Stage in Higher Education Planning*.

- The research universities are becoming research factories. This increases professor recognition and power, the faculty is stronger in the institution due to outside funding.
- The liberal arts colleges are increasing in student numbers. Where the research institutions train specialized investigators, faculty in liberal arts colleges are devoted to the education of students to become well-rounded leaders in society. The faculty at these small colleges are bright, multitalented, and are developing global entrepreneurial programs.
- The array of different types of colleges, i.e., private, technology based, and regional religiously affiliated are required, because of the ever-changing nature of the instruction, to keep changing with the environment.
- Two-year and proprietary schools and under-endowed private colleges take in underprepared students who are adult learners. Planning for different types of delivery (including length of courses) and different types services will be require of the institution to ensure student success.

Keller suggested that educational planners need to rethink their processes, mode of operations and planning. He identified two important perspectives to respond to the dynamic changes in society: (a) the movement beyond "planning" to structural changes and (b) the need to understand that the exact nature of the structural changes depends on the type of institution for which the planning is being done (Keller, p. 63). Researchers agree that planners (leaders) need to be innovative and moderate risk-takers. They serve as policy advisers and decision makers about the future. As such, they need to be stable, effective, influential persons who are self-confident enough to handle the inevitable criticisms that new strategies receive...If university planning is to work, the special qualities of those doing the planning are more important than their representativeness (Goncalves, 1997).

A configuration of higher education planning, using the work of Keller (1999) and others (Goncalves, 1997), focused on an integrative planning model for college and university programs and has been modified from a framework for operations/manufacturing strategy (Hill, 2000). In this study, Hill followed the 4 steps below and changed the "manufacturing strategy" to "program strategy."

1. Objectives for the institution based on external data using tool (SWOT) and (STEP) for environmental scanning to determine the institution's position in the market.
2. Recruiting or marketing strategy: innovation and program variety.
3. Student winners and student qualifiers: Why does a student come to the institution?
4. Program strategy: internal structure and process consistent with student winners and student qualifying criteria.

Research models created for higher educational strategic planning address forces that drive institutions to create formal plans. The external forces are based on the environmental shift of the students seeking higher education. Accrediting organizations, both regional and specialty accrediting bodies, view strategic planning as basic good practice and require that formal plans exist. Assessment of formal educational activities and evaluation of governance and administration, financial stability, admission and student personnel services, resources, student academic achievement, organizational effectiveness, and relationships with outside constituents should be reflected in the strategic plan. A simplified model of strategic planning in business and academics is displayed in Figure 2. This model represents components from the literature models discussed and summarizes the results.

Figure 2. Simplified strategic planning model in business and academics.

This model serves as a starting point for this research study. The purpose of this study was to reveal emerging themes and plausible relationships in the creation and implementation of strategic plans by leaders of the business units. This research explored evidence of actual use of models found in literature, the extent to which they are used, and evidence of the successful implementation by business unit leaders.

As business unit leaders respond to their changing environment and modify the plans, what are the common themes, limitations or gaps in this planning process? What drives the leaders to plan strategically, and are they confident in their planning abilities? With the experience and education of these individuals, what new processes/models will emerge as more effective methods for planning? Within the scope of the process are there barriers, limitations; what really works? These perspectives may help others engage in a more efficient strategic planning process and integration into the institutions' strategic planning process.

CHAPTER 3
METHODOLOGY

A qualitative approach provides an effective mechanism for exploratory research when variables are unknown and when a theory base does not exist for a particular study (Creswell, 1994). A qualitative research study was conducted using an inductive grounded theory approach. Grounded theory is a qualitative method that allows the investigator to systematically collect information about a particular phenomenon and to inductively arrive at a substantive or a formal theory to explain it (Glaser & Strauss, 2008). It permits the discovery of new information with the express purpose of developing a theoretical formulation that explains findings and provides a framework for future exploration (Strauss & Corbin, 1990). Determining whether or not there is a previous speculative discovery provides a theory that "fits or works" in a substantive or formal area (through further testing, clarification, or reformulation is still necessary), since the theory has been derived from data, not deduced from logical assumption (Glaser & Strauss, 2008). Qualitative research provided a way to understand the creative process of the participants derived through personal education and experiences. This understanding permitted the discovery of new information with the express purpose of developing a theoretical formulation related to strategic planning in business units of higher education institutions.

Assumptions and Rationale for Qualitative Methodology

A qualitative approach was the best approach to identify the elements within strategic plan models. Qualitative research can obtain perspectives of the creation, implementation and thoughts pertaining to the phenomenon of a leader's understanding of strategic planning. The grounded theory approach was used to develop plausible relationships among concepts and sets of concepts. This situation is one in which individuals interact, take action, or engage in a process in response to a phenomenon (Creswell, 1998). The researcher, through identification of the strategic planning processes and the limitations of current strategic planning provided a voice for successful academic leaders. The emergent themes and relationships have created a current model for successful plan formulation by leaders in higher education.

This research sought to provide a perspective of the leaders' positions, personal educations, and understanding of the constraints associated with strategic development. Grounded theory was expected to develop theory reflective of the reality of strategic planning by these individuals (Strauss & Corbin, 1990). Building the theory relies on the interpretation of the data, for the data must be conceptualized and the concepts related to form a theoretical rendition of reality. One begins with an area of study, such as strategic planning, and what is relevant to that area will be allowed to emerge (Strauss & Corbin, p.22). The reality of strategic planning does exist in some form, either a structure from business industry or a modified version for academia. The participant's knowledge, internal and external environmental factors was expected to impact the process of creation and implementation of strategic plans.

Collection of qualitative interview data and dissemination of perspective data did lend understanding of the process and the use of the models. Listening to the perspectives of higher education business unit leaders provided a broader and deeper understanding of models and data gathering methods used to successfully implement a strategic plan because each of these leaders had a different view, educational background, and institutional environment. Listening gave these professionals voices regarding the success or inadequacies of the models and processes outlined in the literature. Lessons learned by leaders in the business units was expected to provide a roadmap or process for others in higher education; interpretation of this interview data was expected to contribute to the emergence of new models or modifications of existing models in literature.

Participants

The method for participant selection was consistent with the data collection strategy. The researcher used stratified purposeful sampling to select those individuals to represent particular subgroups of interest (Patton, 1990). Patton (1990) and Merriam (1998) posited that the logic and power of purposeful sampling lies in selecting information-rich cases to study in depth.

Access to the sample population occurred through leaders in business education who are selected from the member institutions of the International Assembly for Collegiate Business Education (IACBE).

The purpose of the IACBE is to promote and recognize excellence in business education in colleges and universities—at both the undergraduate and graduate levels—through specialized accreditation (IACBE, 2006). To be considered by specialty accrediting bodies, like IACBE, regional accreditation is required. Recognition of degrees and acceptance of transfer credit and for the inclusion on the Web for U.S. higher education lists is through the following regional accrediting bodies.

- Middle States Association of Colleges & Schools – Commission on Higher Education (States: DE, DC, MD, NJ, NY, PA, Puerto Rico, & Virgin Islands.
- New England Association of Schools & Colleges – Commission on Institutions of Higher Education (States: CN, MA, ME, NH, RI, VT).
- North Central Association of Colleges & Schools – Higher Learning Commission (States: AZ, AR, CO, IL, IN, IA, KS, MI, MN, MO, NM, NE, ND, OH, OK, SD, WV, WI, WY).
- Northwest Commission on Colleges & Universities (States: AK, ID, MT, NV, OR, UT, WA).
- Southern Association of Colleges & Schools – Commission on Colleges (States: AL, FL, GA, KY, LA, MI, NC, SC, TN, TX, VA)
- Western Association of Schools & Colleges (States: CA, HI, and the Pacific)

Thus, the identification of regional accrediting bodies was important in this study because standards within the scope of this accreditation were expected to impact the strategic planning process of the participating institutions selected for this study. The accrediting bodies likely serve as a driving force and catalyst behind the need for strategic planning in higher education.

Consent was given by the IACBE president to conduct this study with their members. In discussions with the IACBE president and accreditation officer, recommendations for the selection of participants were reviewed. The criteria for selection was: (a) the business leader's positions as the chair, director or dean of their business programs or divisions; (b) the leader's college or university category, as outlined in this section, to obtain a diverse population of institutional types, states, and regional accreditation; and (c) past evidence of their ability to produce exceptional strategic plans of their programs as required by the IACBE. For the five types, non-traditional, private, historically faith based, faith based (Protestant), and faith based (Catholic), the types are outlined and defined in the Table 1.

Table 1

Description of Institution Types by IACBE*

Types	Description
Non-Traditional	Colleges and universities where the business programs are innovative and using non-traditional pedagogy; they are entrepreneurial and market-based.
Private Institutions	Colleges and universities that are non-profit, independently governed institutions.
Historically Faith Based	Colleges and universities founded by a religious order or denomination but is no longer under the authority of the founders.
Faith Based – Protestant	College and universities where faith is overtly integrated in the education process with a Protestant faith based mission.
Faith Based- Catholic	College and universities where faith is overtly integrated in the education process with a Catholic faith based mission.

* International Assembly for Collegiate Business Education (IACBE)

According to Lincoln & Guba (1985), within criterion/purposeful sampling, the size of the sample cannot be predetermined: "The criterion invoked to determine when to stop sampling is informational redundancy, not a statistical confidence level" (p.203). Seidman (1998) proclaimed, "'Enough' is an interactive reflection of every step of the interview process and different for every study and each researcher" (p. 48). Informational redundancy is defined as collecting data until no new information is forthcoming from new sampled units (Merriam, 1998). Patton (1990) recommended specifying a minimum sample size based on expected reasonable coverage of the phenomenon, given the purpose of the study. Seidman (1998) stated: "The method of phenomenological interviewing applied to a sample of participants who all experience similar structural and social conditions gives enormous power to the stories of a relatively few participants" (p. 48). Additionally, researchers (i.e., Merriam, 1998; Patton, 1990; Seidman, 1998) recommended that if no redundancy is found, the researcher should draw assumptions and conclusions from the data collected.

Four individuals from each IACBE institutional type for a total of 20 leaders were interviewed to ensure that strategic planning perceptions of the business leaders were covered in each type.

Creation of Interview Questions

The interview questions were initiated in a pilot study in a qualitative research course in the fall of 2006 and, as recommended by Maxwell (1996), were administered to members of the same potential population. The four participants in the pilot study were selected because of their leadership status in their business units and were members of the board of commissioners for the IACBE. They were also informed that this would only be a pilot study and their responses will not be included in this research study. The pilot process assisted in generation of the final open-ended interview questions and the techniques of collection and dissemination of data. Comments and suggestions from the pilot participants were incorporated into the interview questions. A presentation was also completed to the dissertation committee for approval. The purpose of this review was to offer suggestions to improve the quality of the interview questions and the reduction of researcher bias by infusing the expertise of higher education professionals and not based solely upon the researcher's opinion.

The final interview instrument was created by the researcher following the pilot study and was aligned with the research questions. The open-ended questions were designed in a semi-structured format that allowed the interview to be guided by the issues to be explored; neither the exact wording nor the order of the questions was predetermined (Merriam, 1998).

Contacting the Participants

The scripted communications were prepared for four interviews from each of the five institutional types found in Table 1 (p. 31), for a total of 20 interviews.

The selected participants were contacted to request their participation in the research project via e-mail. They were informed of the type of questions that would be asked; the length of time of the interview, and that their anonymity would be maintained through an assigned code number. Prospective participants were provided the opportunity to accept or decline participation in the study. When interest was verified, the researcher initiated a phone conversation to set up the interview time and to request the consent form. The interviews were set up during a designated time; the individuals were called punctually at the assigned time, and interviewed via phone in their natural setting, a location convenient to the participant.

Data Collection

The researcher collected data from business leaders at IACBE member schools that met the selection criteria (Table 1). Data collection consisted of semi-structured interviews (Strauss & Corbin, 1990) using a set of questions in the interview session with additional probing questions following the lead of the research participant.

Interviews were completed via phone and were not face-to-face for two important reasons. First, the phone interviews facilitated holding the conversation in the leader's natural setting where each had the ability to talk frankly. Second, the researcher's position as a Vice President of Academic Affairs prevented extensive travel to diverse geographic locations; diversity in location was needed to obtain the required depth and breadth of experiences in strategic planning. The questions were not given provided prior to the interview to deter a scripted response. The researcher believed that the spontaneity of responses was important to obtain the reality of their strategic planning processes.

Each participant consented to audio recording the interview. Each interview averaged forty-five to sixty minutes in length. The interviews were only identified as a code number and sequentially delineated by the criteria of school category, state, and regional accreditation body. The interviews were held in a closed-door setting with only the researcher and participant on speaker phones. Interviews were held in the offices of the participants' institution so they might have access to any documents required to assist them in answering the interview questions. The participants were given the option to discontinue the interview at anytime.

The interviews were standardized and predetermined. Open-ended questions were asked in the same order to maintain consistency and to elicit words and images of the process (Creswell, 1998). The open-ended questions were structured to communicate interest and trust in the respondent's judgment, were easily answered, and did not pose a threat to the participants. The responses required probing to gather more information regarding personal education, creation and implementation of their strategic plans, and finally how they were integrated into the institution's plan.

Each interview was tape recorded and then transcribed by the researcher to analyze the data. Tapes were erased immediately after transcription. The researcher used member checks to obtain feedback from research participants regarding the accuracy of transcription, enhancing the validity of the decisions made by the researcher. Additional materials were not requested due to the proprietary and financial information that would be in the institution's strategic plan.

Validity and Reliability

There are several threats to interpretation. Threats to validity can occur as a result of the researcher's own biases and beliefs if the researcher attaches the researcher's own words and meanings to the interviews and observations (Maxwell, 1996). In the instrument design phase, the instrument must be constructed to ensure internal validity and reliability (Soy, 2000). Lincoln & Guba (1981) stressed that the data analysis procedures influence the validity of conclusions drawn. According to Yin (2002), validity can be very difficult to obtain in qualitative research because the researchers have the tendency to infuse their opinions into the study. Internal validity demonstrates that certain conditions lead to other conditions, and requires the use of multiple pieces of evidence from multiple sources to uncover convergent lines of inquiry (Yin, 2000).

To minimize the impact of researcher bias, the researcher conducted a thorough literature review to acquire a full understanding of how strategic planning is completed in academia, business and more specifically in higher education. This verification of information from the literature and the interviews will help to identify additional insight into the understanding, or lack of understanding, of the strategic planning process. Measurement tools and assessment of successful strategic planning were also reviewed. The literature review helped the researcher concentrate on the facts surrounding the academic leaders and their knowledge of strategic planning.

This qualitative research study also incorporated the following strategies to enhance internal validity. Member checks provide an additional method of ensuring description validity (Creswell, 1994; Denzin & Lincoln, 2005). The researcher addressed the member checks by reviewing and discussing, with interviewees, the accuracy of the findings. The interviewees had the opportunity to read the researcher's transcripts, each interviewee was able to validate the results and make any additions or edits to the manuscripts.

Constant communication was conducted with colleagues, researcher's doctoral committee members, academic leaders, and business leaders that shared a common interest in strategic planning. The interview questions were piloted with participant feedback and were also submitted to a panel of experts (dissertation committee) who offered recommendations for improving the instrument. This feedback helped guide the researcher to finalize specific research questions and the appropriate research methodology especially through conversations with the committee members and chairperson.

The primary threat to description validity is an inaccurate representation of what the researcher heard from a research participant (Maxwell, 1996). Qualitative design methods of audio taping interviews and taking detailed, concrete, and chronological field notes during the interview process serve to enhance description validity (Maxwell, 1996). Two additional specific threats to qualitative research validity include researcher bias and reactivity (Maxwell, 1996). Researcher bias occurs when the selection of data fit the researcher's preconceptions (Miles & Huberman, 1994).

Member checks provided an opportunity to consult with each interview participant about the accuracy of the transcripts. This process insured the final document represented the participants' perspectives regarding strategic planning and their institution's strategic planning process.

Reliability refers to the stability, accuracy, and precision of measurement (Soy, 2000), and is defined by Merriam (1998) as the extent to which the study's results can be replicated. Reliability is problematic in social science because human behavior is never static; however, reliability can be increased throughout the study by interviewing participants until the data collected was redundant. Qualitative research requires that the researcher is engaged with the data collection, the analysis and the interpretation; thus, it important for the researcher to relay the information that is obtained by the participants, member check, and code appropriately.

Data Analysis

Glaser & Strauss (2008) emphasized that grounded theory requires the construction of theory. To formulate a theory, the researcher used a systematic coding approach. Merriam (1998) defined coding as assigning some sort of shorthand designation to various aspects of the researcher's data, so that the researcher can easily retrieve specific pieces of the data. Strauss & Corbin (1990) described three different types of coding presented by Borgatti (1997):

1. Open coding: identifying, naming, categorizing and describing instances found within the interview transcripts, field notes from observations, or other documents of meaning by the researcher;

2. Axial coding: the process of relating codes (categories and properties) to each other, via a combination of inductive and deductive thinking. To simplify this process, grounded

theorists emphasize causal relationships by fitting things into a basic frame of generic relationships;

3. Selective coding: process of choosing one category to be the core category, and relating all other categories to that category. The essential idea is to develop a single storyline around which everything else is draped.

Using the constant comparative method to code the interview transcripts, the researcher analyzed each transcript, searching for themes that characterized the links. Merriam (1998) supports the constant comparative method that was developed by Glaser & Strauss (1967) as a means to develop grounded theory. This inductive process illustrates working back and forth between the themes and the database until the researcher has established a comprehensive set of themes. The most important point in the coding literature was to bring out the participant's meaning, not the researcher's meaning, of the problem or issue (Creswell, 2009).

The researcher began with a particular occurrence from an interview and compared the answer in the same set of data or in another category like the participant institutional types found in Table 1. These comparisons led to possible categories that were then compared to each other and to other occurrences. Comparisons were constantly made within and between levels of conceptualization until a theory could be formulated (Glaser & Straus, 2008).

Recommendations by Merriam (1998) were followed by analyzing the transcripts of the interviews for similarities of occurrences. This process was characterized by axial coding where the researcher related codes (categories and properties) to each other through a combination of inductive and deductive reasoning. Once the themes were determined, the themes were correlated to the research questions. The following is an example of how this was accomplished during analysis of an interview transcript.

The researcher was able to determine what type of education and experience influenced the academic leaders to have the knowledge and skills to create strategic planning for their units. Responses reflected, "Education gave me the foundation, but I really did not learn strategic planning until I had to apply it on the job," or "No education can prepare you for strategic planning in higher education, the model is different somehow." From these occurrences, the property, *'prepared,'* was developed that described the theme. With this information, the researcher formulated a hypothesis that connected the link to its property: "*All higher education business unit leaders must make plans for their programs, strategic or not. How they learned this function might be from education or experience in the corporate world."* This hypothesis was constantly compared with data collected throughout the interviews.

According to Glaser & Strauss (1967), and reaffirmed by Merriam (1998), the development of categories, properties, and tentative hypotheses through the constant comparative method, is a process whereby the data gradually evolves into a core of emerging theory. Byrne (2001) stated that the core usually has some of the following characteristics: 1) recurs frequently, 2) links various data, 3) has an explanatory function, 4) has an implication for formal theory, and 5) becomes more detailed. Finally, once the researcher finished coding and interpreting the data, a comprehensive review of each case was written.

Ethical Considerations

Ethical considerations for the participants of the study were a concern. The researcher's intention was to promote a trustful relationship with all participants to enable precise, rich information without negative impacts on the interviewees. In the initial contact with the interviewees, an informed consent for research participation that included ethical concerns was given to each of the participants. The researcher requested a signature to verify the participant's understanding. This document assured that participation of the interviewees was entirely voluntary and names would not be revealed.

Participants were also informed that they could refuse to answer any question or withdraw from the interview at any time. All data collected became the property of the researcher, and excerpts from the interviews were part of the final research study.

A code number was given to each transcript. Participants were also reassured that they would be able to review the transcripts of their interviews for accuracy. Additionally, permission was received from the University of Nebraska, Lincoln Institutional Review Board for Research to conduct research on human subjects.

Summary of Methodology

This study was designed to explore the perceptions of higher education business unit leaders about the creation and implementation of strategic plans across five types of institutions; non-traditional; private; historically faith-based; faith based Protestant; and faith-based Catholic institutions.

Few studies have approached this dilemma from a qualitative perspective. According to scholars (i.e., Glaser & Strauss, 1967; Merriam, 1998; Seidman, 1998), qualitative research seizes the opportunity to understand the experiences of people and the meaning they make of that experience. Grounded theory is a qualitative methodology that derives theory through the experiences and perceptions of human subjects. Therein lies a possibility to create a new model for strategic planning creation and to assist these leaders in the implementation of a successful plan. What are the best practices of these leaders, what are the limitations and what makes the strategic plan a success?

Twenty higher education business unit leaders were interviewed and information was discovered regarding the creation, implementation and measured outcomes of their plans. In addition, data was gathered to understand how their education and experience had prepared them to apply their skills. Interviews were the main source of data collection, and the data was analyzed using the constant comparative method. The constant comparative method was developed in concurrence with grounded theory as a way to compare findings within the data throughout the research process. The result of the analysis produced a rich description of the leader's experiences and rationale for their decisions to create and implement strategic plans. These models may change as further research follows the grounded theory approach to develop plausible relationships among concepts and sets of concepts...this situation is one in which individuals interact, take actions, or engage in a process in response to a phenomenon (Creswell, 1998).

These responses began to take on emergent themes. Grounded theory, the most widely known inductive approach, was described by Strauss & Corbin (1990) as "discovered, developed, and provisionally verified through systematic data collection and analysis" (p.23). This process of data analysis in grounded theory, taking data collection to emerging categories, referred to as constant comparative method of analysis, is both rigorous and systematic.

Examples are provided with each category placed in matrices, including summarized quotes from the interviews. Initially, themes began to emerge and were labeled by using the topic of the questions but quickly expanded to subcategories or divergence from the initial concept by *in vivo* codes or the words and phrases used by the informants themselves, catchy ones that immediately draw attention (Glaser, 1978).

The next step in this systematic process is *axial coding*. Where open coding fractures the data and allows one to identify some categories, their properties, and dimensional location, axial coding puts those data back together in new ways by making connections between categories and subcategories (Strauss & Corbin (1990, p.97). In grounded theory these subcategories are now linked to the subcategories. This connection from the systematic approach beginning with the occurrence of a phenomenon or main category then relating the context or a specific set of properties or actions or subcategories, begins to pull the open coding back together again through interaction and outcomes of that interaction. When linking the open coding and axial coding it is a complex analysis, in fact, it is performing four distinct analytical steps almost simultaneously which includes the relationship of subcategories to a category by means of statements denoting the nature of the relationship between them and the phenomenon (Strauss, p. 107).

The final step in analysis was integration of categories to form a grounded theory; this is done through selective coding. Selective coding is used to build a story that connects the category relationships and systematically develops a picture of reality and validates the emergent theory against the data which grounds the theory. Coding is linking rather than merely labeling. It leads you from the data to the idea and from the idea to all the data pertaining to that idea (Morris, 2002). The grounded theory is presented as a visual diagram showing the relationships among concepts.

CHAPTER 4

DEMOGRAPHICS

The purpose of this qualitative study was to reveal the perspectives of higher education business unit leaders in academic business units/divisions and their ability to create and implement strategic plans. These individuals, who have been exposed in either their educational or experiential background to the models and practices of strategic planning, were expected to have skills and expertise in pulling together effective strategic plans for their units and ultimately integrate with their institutional plan. The researcher interviewed 20 academic business leaders who represented five types of institutions as defined by the International Assembly for Collegiate Business Education (IACBE), see Table 1.

As outlined in the data analysis section of Chapter 3, the qualitative analysis was used to compare occurrences found within transcripts of interviews. The researcher transcribed the taped interviews and then coded the data by reading transcripts line-by-line. The researcher identified themes by uncovering rich informative responses from the interviewees. Themes are supported by direct quotes of the interviewees. This analysis is presented and addressed in Chapter 5.

Demographics and Participant Characteristics

Initial questions, demographic in nature, were asked of each interviewee to determine (a) the size of the institution and business unit, (b) the regional accrediting body associated with the institution, (c) the education and experience of the business leader, and (c) the current title held. Table 2 displays the institutional demographics and information regarding the participants' education and influence of career experiences. Student count information has impact on the responses associated with the creation and implementation of their strategic plans within the business unit as well as the institution. All participants have a number of years of experience in corporate business or educational administration.

Summary of Demographics

All of the participants held a masters degree either in education or in a business related field. All participants have either obtained a doctoral degree or are currently pursuing the degree. One participant held a Jurist Doctorate and recently decided to step down from an administrative role to faculty.

Comparing the 20 institutions, 17 of the twenty institutions (85%) had an institutional student count under 10,000 students with an average institutional student count of 2,876. The remaining three institutions (15%) averaged 31,333 total students. The researcher assumed that institutional size would have an impact on the strategic planning process.

For the set of 20 institutions, the size of the business units averaged 1,441 student cou nt. This is an expected number as the majority of schools that are members and accredited by the IACBE are smaller business colleges and universities. The statistics for the regional accrediting bodies of the 20 institutions were as follows:

Four participants were members of the Middle States Association of Colleges & Schools – Commission on Higher Education. Regional Accrediting Body abbreviations: North Central Association – NCA; North Eastern Association – NEA; Middle States –MS; Western Association - WA

Table 2

Demographics and Participant Characteristics

IACBE Category	Institution Student Count	Business Unit Student Count	Regional	Education	Experience	Current Title
Non-Traditional	45,000	8,500	NCA	PhD – Org Behavior, HR, MS – Org Behavior & HR College Professor	Corporate Org Behavior	Chair Graduate School of Management
	35,000	900	NCA	PhD- Higher Education and Leadership MS Logistics	Sales and Marketing	Dean – MBA program
	7,500	2,625	NCA	PhD- Higher Education MS Educational Admin	Management in healthcare	Associate Provost
	3,500	140	NCA	JD Law	Corporate Law VPAA Professor	Department head, returned to FT faculty
Private	14,000	7,000		DBA MBA- major accounting	Credit analyst-Banking, Accountant adjunct	Associate Dean

IACBE Category	Institution Student Count	Business Unit Student Count	Regional	Education	Experience	Current Title
Private (cont'd)	3600	800	MS	ABD MS- Political Science	College instructor City planner	Dean – School of Business
	2600	635	NCA	JD – Law MBA MA- Org Development	Corporate Law Healthcare	Dean – School of Business
	800	236	NCA	Working on PhD in Finance MBA	Financial Analyst Software Adjunct	Chair – Business Department
Faith Based Catholic	5,000	1300	NCA	PhD – Higher Education Leadership MBA	Merchandise Buyer, store Adjunct faculty	Chair, Department of Business
	3,200	1575	NCA	PhD – Business Finance, Accounting, and IS MS – Education	CPA Firm	Dean of Business and Technology
	2,500	260	MS	PhD – Economics MS – Economics	College Professor Economic advisor	Chair, Department of Business
	2,300	425	MS	PhD – Higher Education and Leadership MBA MS HR Management	CPA in Corporate University Administration – consultant	Dean – Business School
Historically Faith Based	1,200	300	NCA	PhD – Business MBA	Corporate HR College professor	Chair, Business Dept.

IACBE Category	Institution Student Count	Business Unit Student Count	Regional	Education	Experience	Current Title
Historically Faith Based(cont.)	1,000	400	NCA	Working on PhD in Finance MBA – Accounting	Controller Teaching 5th year	Assistant Professor and Director
	824	100	NCA	Working on PhD in Education MS –Healthcare Business	Health Information Management Instructor business	Director-Healthcare Business
	669	200	NEA	DBA MBA	Fast food manager Officer rural Bank	Chair, Business Division
Non-Traditional	7,500	2000	NCA	PhD – Management MBA – Finance	Corporate Controller	Dean, Graduate Programs
	3,200	700	MS	PhD – Administration Policy MS – Math	Junior High Math Teacher Public Accounting	Dean, School of Business
	2,000	230	NCA	PhD – Economics MBA – Accounting	19 years higher education	Chair Business Division
	1,500	500		Working on PhD in Education & MBA	College Professor and Admin	Chair, Business

- Two participants were members of the New England Association of Schools & Colleges – Commission on Institutions of Higher Education

- Twelve participants were members of North Central Association of Colleges & Schools – Higher Learning Commission.

- No participants were members of Northwest Commission on Colleges & Universities.

- No participants were members of Southern Association of Colleges & Schools – Commission on Colleges.

- One participant was a member of the Western Association of Schools & Colleges.

Participant Educational and Experiential Preparation

When the participants were asked if their education and/or experience prepared them for their leadership role and especially the requirement of strategic planning, the majority of the participants answered favorably. This self-evaluation was one of the first questions asked by the researcher and the response illustrated their perceived abilities. Participants were confident the skills, either obtained during their education or experience, were adequate to be successful in their academic roles and their ability to create effective strategic plans. Tables 3a and 3b illustrate the responses of preparation, both educational (3a) and experiential (3b), for their academic role and more specifically the participant's perceived ability to create and implement a strategic plan.

Table 3a

Participant Educational Preparation

IACBE Category	Participant 1	Participant 2	Participant 3	Participant 4
Non-Traditional	- nothing in my education background - yes on the job training.	- not education - not trained or prepared to be an academic administrator	- both education and experience	- education some skill building in my PhD program.
Private	- nothing on education	- both - mostly experience	- experiential learning.	- education foundation - more so the application has been from experience
Historically Faith Based	- education helped me the most.	Nothing on education	Nothing on education	- both
Faith Based Catholic	- nothing in my academic back ground	- yes, the MBA for the business part and the education leadership	- coursework helps, it gives me a framework.	- none in education
Faith Based Protestant	-education management oriented	- good preparation, especially in my MBA.	- both my education and experience	- education specifically MBA

Table 3b

Participant Experiential Preparation

IACBE Category	Participant 1	Participant 2	Participant 3	Participant 4
Non-Traditional	- corporate experience	- experience - professional development skills	- experience in higher education	- experience 30 years
Private	- experience of 30 years in business	- experience	- experience	- both - knowing the institution
Historically Faith Based	- experience in higher education	- experience	- experience	- more experience
Faith Based Catholic	- I think that business and business related faculty understand how organizations work;	- accrediting body IACBE	- experience	- experience
Faith Based Protestant	- No strategic planning experience in corporate	- experience	- current experience	- academia and learn from my administrators

All participants indicated they were able to lead in their academic role and create strategic plans, and the researcher characterized all participants to be *"confident"* either through their education or experience. The researcher found the knowledge obtained through the experience of the participants was stronger than that obtained through their education.

The educational preparation was mixed; of the 20 participants, 8 reported that they received no formal education or training in strategic planning, and they were educated in their own specific disciplines. Four of these 8 participants expressed various levels of frustration with both their lack of strategic planning and their global management skills. The remaining 4 participants had no response to education as they commented only on their knowledge gained from experience. The knowledge gained through education is a foundation for the participants to function in their leadership career. The majority began their careers as faculty and progressed to administrative roles because their experience was noted by institutional administration.

One participant commented on his role as an administrator, "My education did not train me for my administrative role, on the job training did. There was nothing in my education background that would have prepared me for academic leadership."

In addition the following three leaders acknowledged their Ph.D. preparation and outlined the need for more administrative skill building. All three alluded to the program's academic and research orientation.

(Leader 1) academic preparation is academic and my role now is principally administrative. So, there is nothing in my academic background that was preparatory for the administrative tasks.

This participant discussed the need for additional management courses in their Ph.D. program orientation,

(Leader 2) It would have been nice if my Ph.D. program would have been a little more management oriented. There were some courses that had parts of it but it would have been great to have courses in human resources, strategic planning and just more management classes, but it was more on evaluation and legal aspects of higher education.

Another participant echoed this focus on research and not administration skills in their doctoral program.

(Leader 3) My doctoral program was traditional research, not geared toward administration or teaching. Some of my research is in leadership, so, content wise I was aware and informed of management and leadership but I was not trained or prepared to be an academic administrator.

This knowledge gained through education was viewed as a foundation to understand planning and management of operations, stating their education was primarily business oriented. All participants were confident in their educational background and their ability to lead and to achieve the goals and objectives of the strategic plan they organized. Specific statements were given by the leaders depicting this preparation: "Does education prepare anyone for their role? [laughter]. I think I received pretty good preparation, especially in my MBA."

One leader commented on his positive skill building in his Ph.D. program, *"My Ph.D. focused on the leadership perspective, technology; [it] addressed market changes and how to position yourself. Both education and experience have prepared me."*

Another cited the foundational skills in their educational background, *"Obviously, with my education, the textbook allows me to understand the importance of strategic planning, but more so the application has been from my experience at the institution where we do run as a strategic business."*

The researcher assumed that the participants' education would play a significant role in gaining the knowledge and skills to plan strategically. In contrast to the educational background, an overwhelming 100% of all participants reported that they had learned more either on the job in their current positions or through corporate business applications.

The following participants commented that a combination of both experience and education was important: *"More so the application has been from my experience at the institution where we do run as a strategic business."*

This participant cited the knowledge of the institution and organizational structure as an important component in forming the strategic plans,

I think it is a combination, the most important component is here at my institution where I have had most of the strategic planning, knowing the institution and the organization is very important, know your mission and how you can strategically plan. Our institution is a private, not for profit, but we do run as a strategic business.

Statements validating the business experience were observed for several participants. The statement below articulates many of the same statements for the majority of study participants.

Well, my experience of 30 years in business gives me a basic approach of what I would characterize as an operating philosophy as opposed to a scholarly research philosophy. Our school is not heavy into research, it is a teaching institute designed and appealing to students who are preparing for careers. So, my orientation fits well with the mission of the business school and the mission of the institution.

One participant elaborated on the experience in business and thus having an advantage over colleagues at the institution,

I have an advantage over many of my colleagues in other disciplines that don't know how to do strategic planning, outcomes assessment, budgeting . . . because of my background that has helped me a lot. I have done consulting in the business area and helped other universities and other schools.

Summary of Participant Educational and Experiential Preparation

The additional pressures of cost constraints, public accountability, and increased regulation and faculty shortages in some areas have added to the complexity of higher education. Within this framework, there has been a growing need to recast the academic leader as a business officer first, who also understands and encourages faculty development and growth. . .building consensus for effective planning and decision making and designing quality programs which respond to student and community needs (Seagren et al., 1994).

The researcher assumed the participants' education and experience in business would be a key factor in their level of confidence in the creation of strategic planning. Surprisingly, skills were strongly linked to experience rather than to educational knowledge. Evidence from the participants' interviews verified this assumption.

Participants expressed the view that their continued work toward a good strategic plan within their business departments would help in the integration of strategic planning in the institution, and the majority of participants responded that they have an advantage over their colleagues in understanding and implementation of strategic plans.

Demographics of the institutions and characteristics of the participants provided a foundational view of the institutions and the participants. The results of the research questions will be summarized from the data obtained and analyzed by the researcher. Further discussion of participant responses and emergent themes will be shown in Chapter 5.

CHAPTER 5
GROUNDED THEORY STORYLINE

The story line, for grounded theory development, is within "each section" of this chapter. The researcher begins with open-coding occurrences from each interview. These responses are then placed in tables to assist with the axial coding process relating the responses and assigning themes within the International Assembly for Collegiate Business Education (IACBE) types. The tables were based on emergent themes for each research question. All research questions are answered at the end of this chapter.

The participants were questioned regarding their limitations/challenges and their responses to what would enhance their strategic planning process were the two final research questions. Since these two final research questions directly affected emergent themes among the model structure, the limitations/challenges and enhancements were analyzed within the sections to give more depth to the responses and to show impact on the emergent grounded theory model.

At the conclusion of each section a summary showing the category comparisons and conceptualization of theory formulation was developed. The researcher then began to build a story-line and visual model of each section with an overall grounded theory model presenting the emergent themes.

Section I: Accountability and Transparency

The purpose of this qualitative study was to reveal the perspectives of higher education business unit leaders in academic business units/divisions and their ability to create and implement strategic plans. The research question was addressed in this section, *"What drives the need for strategic planning in the institution and business units?"*

In the literature review for this study, significant findings from the Spellings Commission Report suggested that planning was less than fully effective in higher education. As part of the six principles within the Spellings Commission, accountability and transparency of the institutions may increase the role of the accrediting bodies requiring some type of planning (Ruben et al., 2008). These two directives of accountability and transparency drives the creation of strategic plans and provides direction, goal achievement, and information to all stakeholders.

The accountability and transparency of colleges and universities has become part of the fabric of higher education and will continue to be in the future. Creation of a strategic plan is designed to provide direction, goal achievement, and information to the institution, programs and other stakeholders. Participants were asked what they perceived to be the driving forces, both internal and external factors, to create a strategic plan for their business unit. In addition, to these driving forces, participation in the creation and communication of the plan addressed the transparency and input to the plan.

Internal driving forces for the higher education business unit leaders in this study were found to be primarily (a) the direction of executive administration and (b) the mission of the institution.

The review of literature revealed external drivers to strategic planning as primarily regional accrediting bodies. In contrast to the literature, external driving forces in this study were found to be (a) market penetration and (b) competition to remain a viable institution. Specialty accreditation, like IACBE, also played a motivational role in the business leader's strategic plan creation. Participants perceived minimal motivation from the regional accrediting bodies.

In the majority of institutions, the lack of transparency to the community where both internal and external publication and information was not divulged and internal communication was also limited.

External Driving Forces

Perceptions of external driving forces among participants of this study were mixed and did not correlate with any of the five IACBE types of institutions. Instead, there were common responses associated with these questions across all institutional types. The researcher did not suggest internal or external forces when engaging the participants; nor were the findings of The Spellings Commission Report suggested as a motivator. The questions addressed only the individuals' perceptions of what drives them personally to strategically plan for their business units in their own institutions.

Several participants suggested the significance of accreditation, specifically IACBE, as the external driving force to plan strategically. The IACBE not only drove the need for strategic planning in some of institutions; it also validated it and encouraged the participants to excel in the process, providing a model to assist in that endeavor.

Advocates of the IACBE responded:

IACBE biggest driving force and modeled our plan from the IACBE. If we didn't have the accreditation, we probably would not have a written business strategic plan.

It was driven by our accrediting bodies, IACBE was ahead of the other programs in the College, it was originally done for IACBE and then for our regional North Eastern Association. We had a rough plan but IACBE was the driving force to put it in writing.

IACBE focuses our efforts on assessment coupled by budgeting; no one (in our institution) is doing this better than business.

There were two participants that did not respond that the specialty accreditation was a driving force, however, it was required and did validate the planning the business departments already accomplished:

Accreditation is not really a driving force. We are doing it anyway; IACBE just encourages it as a part of accreditation.

Accreditation (IACBE) compels us to be more thorough, but really doesn't drive it, reinforces and validates it.

In addition responses to regional accrediting bodies varied as driving forces; most were geared toward institutional strategic planning and maintaining accreditation and not specifically to the business unit.

Middle States I would say that they are a driving force for the University. There is no doubt that the gold standard is the regional accreditation, and without it, you would sink. So, we are very geared to keeping our accreditation that drives us University wide.

Institutionally the regional's (NCA) play a bigger part but not much for the business unit. We would strategic plan anyway; that puts us on a level playing field to be competitive and most institutions in NCA have to.

Other participants specified that the regional accrediting bodies were not a driving force for strategic planning:

Not at that time [regional's]. At that time it was an IACBE driven effort.

In my case for the business unit, the regional's would be a very, very small part of it. Institutionally, it would certainly be a bigger part.

An interesting phenomenon occurred in this section. One regional accrediting body, North Central Association (NCA), was mentioned for having two types of accreditation processes. In further research, the NCA provided two programs for maintaining accredited status: the Program to Evaluate and Advance Quality (PEAQ) and the Academic Quality Improvement Program (AQIP). PEAQ employs a five-step comprehensive evaluation process to determine continued accredited status on a ten year basis. The Academic Quality Improvement Program (AQUIP) infuses the principles and benefits of continuous improvement into the culture of colleges and universities by providing an alternative process through which an institution, already accredited, can maintain its accreditation from the Higher Learning Commission. With AQIP, an institution demonstrates it meets accreditation standards and expectations through sequences of events that align with those ongoing activities that characterize organizations striving to improve their performance (*Handbook of Accreditation Standards*, 2003). AQIP, similar to the early 1991literature, depicted Total Quality Management (TQM) which emerged as a tactical tool for developing corporate strategy and to achieve goals successfully. The relationship between Total Quality Management (TQM) and strategic planning is seen as a key competitive factor, however, quality was allowed to become an incidental and secondary factor, if considered at all in the formulation of a competitive strategy (Leonard & McAdam, 2001).

This process, if chosen by the institution, was a significant driving force in the development of a strategic plan for the entire institution down to the business units. The participants did perceive they were ahead of other areas of their institutions and easily participated in the quality improvement planning. In several interviews, participants responded that their business units had a competitive edge with planning and continuous improvements for their academic programs and ultimately for their institution. Many of the participants mentored other members of the institutions on the process of strategic planning. Significant responses to AQIP stated, "I would say that our university and college of business is way ahead of the curve when all this started. Our university has just recently bought into AQIP with North Central and the outcomes assessment focus there."

Another leader concurred, with emphasis on the institutional leadership recognizing the need for strategic planning and continued improvement, not necessarily driven by AQIP.

Yes, we work closely with the higher learning commission, and again, we actually [are] one of the leading institutions that are starting the AQIP process (NCA) where instead of having every 7 or 10 year site visit for your audit, we are working more toward the continual improvements. So I don't think we do it because we have to (emphasis added); I feel it is more that they help us do it, and the leadership recognizes that we need to.

The major focus of external drivers for all participants, regardless of category, was market analysis and the need to remain competitive in that market. Strong opinions of market penetration emerged as the number one external force among all participants to create a strategic plan. The market perspective was illustrated in different forms, but all related to revenue generation. The first was enrollment of students, *"I think they [accreditation] drive it in a general sense, in that you need to get a certain amount of students and you need to provide all the services for X amount of students."*

Enrollment management and with the addition of course offerings, *"We are constantly driven [in the market] to provide as many courses as students want to take so we have a very strong enrollment management group and you might even call them sales to be honest."*

This participant spoke of enrollment, economic trends and competition as key elements in external drivers,

Well, the external forces I think, [are] competition and socio demographic trends that affect our marketplace so much. I think those are the major external factors. You know so many schools chasing the students in the marketplace, since there are so many suppliers of business education in the marketplace. And in terms of the demand side, the demographics drive a lot of the marketplace in terms of returning adult students to graduate programs and traditional age students to undergraduate programs, so I think those are the main external forces, competition and socio demographic and now with the stock market debacle, there are economic trends affecting us.

The need for consistent market penetration and the need for tuition money to remain viable were acknowledged by these participants.

We do have a consultant that does on-going market research in terms of specialized programming, so it ties in as private institution. We don't have any state support, so our tuition dollars are the prime source of our revenue.

We don't want to change a lot, but I think that if we become more financially insecure, I think you would see us do more SP and development.

One participant commented on the market perspective differently and addressed the competition of particular skills by the employers and demands of careers in the market.

I think we are a career focused institution, preparing our students for getting right out there and using those particular skills, so I think the demands of the careers are out there as the external forces determining what programs we offer.

Internal Driving Forces

If, in fact, external forces, such as market trends and accreditation, drive the need for strategic planning, the implementations of student learning outcomes drivers are "internally" best for the institution. The primary internal driving force for strategic planning was found to be the executive administrations that drive the creation of the plan. Overall, the participants reported that administration (presidential, vice president, deans and directors) drove the planning process and change in the institutions.

Leadership driving the mission of the institution was an overwhelming response in all institutional types. The ability for the executive administration to focus their skills in driving the strategic plans, both institutionally and in the business unit, was the most frequent response to internal drivers,

Our President is an aggressive institutional planner. And so we start from the general institutional plan consisting of published annual goals and an objectives sheet, which is an annual revision to a 5-year strategic plan. So, we work within that context and our planning is kind of a mix of things . . . part of it is responses to the assessments of student learning so it is curriculum driven.

The administrative expectations of strategic planning ground what you do.

The institution culture and the background of senior administrators help to increase accountability.

Vision and culture of the organization, either through current administration or tradition, was also a factor for the participants:

We have a mission-focused management who believe in quality improvement I don't think we do it because we have to, it is more that they help us do it and we recognize that we need to, it is the culture of the institution.

The driver that comes to mind is tradition . . . it [strategic planning] is just something we have believed in so there is an internal feeling that it is useful. Probably the tradition and the usefulness are the main driving forces. You don't want to do things as in the past that you don't feel have been useful.

A vision of 2014, were we want to be as an institution, developed university plan first then our business strategic plan.

In addition to identifying the administration as an internal driving force, the participants emphasized the allocation of limited resources, which includes the business units [This is reviewed in more depth in Section III: budget implications]. Because budget allocation was percieved as a driving force, responses were affected in this section with comparative analysis to budget implications. [A commonality in this sub-category driving force was on-going resource allocation or with a major development area]. There were strong perspectives of this driver in capital funding; one leader had this to say,

Driven by a capital funding drive, foundations want to see that you are planning and that you are thinking ahead. We know we have certain things to accomplish as an institution, so we know we have to plan for the future because we do not have the resources to do all things.

Allocation of limited resources were a concern of a number of participants, not correlated with any particular category; one participant was very succinct:

13 departments vying for limited resources with other schools, additional facilities and faculty are needed to be competitive. If we teach strategic planning in the business school; we ought to practice what we preach and give attention for strategy in the future.

Participation and Publication

The transparency in an institution had a number of definitions and perceptions from administration and accreditation constituents. The Spellings Commission (2006) alluded to the "robust culture of accountability and transparency" that should be cultivated throughout higher education. This transparency would include gathering and maintaining information of comparable information on other colleges and universities. It would also focus on greater input from student learning assessment and external constituents. The meaning for the purpose of this study was simply "Who are the participants in the creation of the strategic plan and what data is gathered for input and review?" The second issue was transparency to the public.

All participants concluded that participation was primarily within their business team including the leader, staff and faculty with limited input from adjunct faculty. Participants commented on the participation of the strategic plan creation. The first three responses were favorable and included entire departments in the planning team: *"Basically, our whole internal team – and that would include all of our full time faculty and staff. We also have input, on a limited basis, from our adjunct faculty."* Departmental retreats were also mentioned,

> *I get an inventory (or SWOT) from everyone individually and try to get it into a written strategic planning form and then share with faculty and staff at a planning retreat in August. We recast the priorities and maybe even eliminate some and focus on the priority for the school.*

One participant reflected on the faculty,

> *I am blessed with a handful of good senior level faculty members, and I'll put drafts on paper, share it with them, and when we seem to have it [plan] in pretty good shape, we share it with the entire department. So, everybody gets a piece of the action and, of course, it then goes forward to the VPAA and then to the president.*

Even though participants may use external constituents such as advisory boards to provide input to the plan, varying degrees of participation and information were reported. Advocates to the idea of external input had this to say regarding external constituents:

> *Every single one of our divisions has an advisory board that helps them to determine things like, "Do we need to made changes in our program?" "What are we preparing our students for?" "What are the career opportunities?" Those types of things. The Deans work with those boards along with the faculty and gather information to take it to corporate.*

Even institutional committees were seen,

> *We do have an advisory board that is made up of business professionals in our geography and student representation is on the board. From the college standpoint, we do seek outside input as well. There is a committee that is an external focused committee.*

Some participants were not as confident in the input of the constituents, one stated,

> *In varying degrees we have had input from our advisory boards to the process. The external communities is hit and miss, they are just not connected in what we are doing.*

Another said, *"We have an advisory board but have not gotten them involved in strategic planning."*

Student input came from outcomes assessment measurements in the form of surveys or from representation on committees. As with the advisory board input, not all student input was solicited. If input was requested, minimal information was shared regarding the strategic plan. Some students were solicited only indirectly through surveys and outcomes assessment measurements:

> *Students input we get through the assessment process; we get them involved in areas of improvement.*

> *There is significant input from our outcomes assessment work which would include input from alumni and students. So, we use our assessment as a major input to the plan and process. I have not considered external constituents for the strategic plan; that is probably a good idea.*

Some participants only ask for student input for certain phases of the process,

> *We involve students and ask them about curriculum and other elements. We do not talk with them about asset reallocation or new programs.*

> *Students are very vocal, even in the non-traditional environment where they are not around a lot; email inoculates them from being polite, and so they will tell you what they think. That feedback comes through a very heavily asynchronous online environment for our MBA courses.*

One participant did use students in focus groups, *"We did do some focus groups with students early on, but as far as the formal development of the plan, they were not involved."*

Only two of the 20 participants regularly used advisory input, professionals in the field, and student input as a standard practice. As a note, these responses were both participants in the Faith Based - Catholic category.

We do have an advisory board that is made up of business professionals in our geography and student representation is on the board. From the College standpoint we do seek outside input as well. There is a committee that is an external focused committee.

We continually involve our advisory board on curriculum changes; changes in the market and especially the strategic plan. Student and alumni representation is part of that group. We also obtain information from our outcomes assessment through student surveys as input to our strategic plan.

Limitations and Enhancements of Participation

The "primary" limitation expressed by the participants for future planning efforts was seen in the participation and education of those involved in the strategic plan process. The majority of the participants expressed that the enhancement to the process would be the need for more faculty, student, and external constituency involvement. The involvement of internal members of the business unit was the most important factor for "buy-in" and acceptance of the plan for successful implementation and outcomes. This limitation was seen among the five types of IACBE schools. Thus it was not a function of the type of institutional process structure, top-down or bottom-up.

Participants commented on the need for education as a foundation to obtain buy-in from all personnel involved. One stated,

When you allow input from everyone and you have a large institution and even distance challenges, there is a complexity to it that you would not find in an institution with centralized departments. We also really need to educate all people in the institution and the departments on the planning process.

Another stated,

One of the challenges, is faculty recruitment and involvement in the planning process. It would be difficult to substantially improve it [strategic planning] without greater knowledge and experience, and even greater motivation of the faculty, unless one or two that are willing to do the whole thing themselves. That would be difficult. I would need to have faculty with more planning experience.

The education of the planning process for all constituents would also help to make the plan less threatening to them for fear of downsizing:

If people were education and knew the process up front, they would not feel threatened by it. They would not be worried that we were going to get rid of faculty because we were going into new areas. Everyone was involved in the grassroots level, and people were assured that the plan was not a threat for downsizing.

Participants expressed that if more involvement by the administration to educate the constituents on the strategic planning process would help to get more people involved. Vision and direction from the executive administration played a significant role:

The biggest limitation to develop a strategic plan was the need to get buy in; we need more direction from management. We need to understand what it is they want us to do with priorities and direction. Right now, it doesn't seem we get a lot of that.

I would like to see [the strategic plan] generated within the department first, then flow up. Ours was top-down, so we got buy-in at the end. I am not sure the buy-in really exists, if you get buy-in at the end. But I think that it would be a stronger plan, if we had more folks creating the plan.

Collaboration with management to understand focus and consensus with incremental victories would help to engage faculty and staff in the business units:

You almost have to manage expectations from the beginning, and you have to give all of the academic units an opportunity to celebrate small victories. You know they won't get everything they want, but maybe there is something very meaningful that could get funded, that would motivate them to engagement in the process.

Some leaders focused their enhancement efforts on student learning outcome assessment. This is important in bottom-up models that put considerable effort in their units to measure successful outcome assessment plans in their areas. Commitment from the faculty was the same for the outcomes process:

I think just trying to get faculty to commit to outcomes assessment for the students. I would feel much more confident that we were really assessing our students accurately, and development and planning would come out of that assessment to the success of our students.

Time and participation to the learning outcomes, this is my next hurdle to get faculty buy-in to this idea of the culture of outcomes and strategic planning; the integration of efforts into planning for the school of business is a challenge.

The participants placed limited involvement of students and external constituencies as an important enhancement for future success of their plans. Participants also wanted to see more participation in the creation of the strategic plan by students and alumni as external constituents. Input to the strategic planning process was seen as a factor in the external environmental scanning:

Alumni after graduation could become more involved in the planning process.

I would like to involve student more in the process and focus on their perspective and what they have learned through outcomes.

I would like to involve student more in the process and advisory board members actively in the process. Also, focus more on student learning outcomes.

I would like to have a more formal process to get students more involved in the strategic plan, maybe some of our upper level or graduate students.

The second portion of the accountability and transparency questioning was asked regarding the publication of their business strategic plan or the institutional strategic plan. The definition of "published" was processed differently by all participants. However, all of the participants either sent the document directly to their administration (academic officer or provost) or some posted on the internet but did comment that it was either not updated or was not read on a consistent basis. There were only two external publications, one was to the IACBE and one participant posted on the Web but was not sure if it was current.

Institutionally, participants did not share information with other areas of the institution and remained in silos of expertise. The literature search revealed that these were consistent issues that plague higher education including: the complex structure of colleges and universities based on traditions and individual silos of expertise; failure to adapt to new environmental demands while assessing internal achievement, which makes it difficult to pull together a formalized strategic plan (Bryson, 1996). This fortunately was found only with one of the participants, *"We do not share the strategic plan amongst the other departments. Quite honestly, I have enough to do with my department; I don't need to read all the other plans."*

Others communicated their plans to the administration and were available either on the Web page to external constituents or on the intranet of the institution; all were required to be sent to the IACBE:

It is communicated to the Provost, and, yes, it is essentially published on our intranet.

It is available, and it is placed on the institutional effectiveness Web page, our is posted there, but I will tell you that we don't do a good job of the keeping stuff updated. . .I think the strategic plan is up to date, but I am not sure if it is posted there.

I know that all of the officers and the administrative cabinet see it. Let me see, yes, we do because, once a year, the president sends that out to the entire faculty and staff.

Yes, we report to our internal and [to our] external to IACBE. Informally, we publish within our institution.

Summary Section I: Accountability and Transparency

Once a sanctuary for unfettered creation of ideas and opinions, colleges and universities have been opened to the play of competitive market forces and the scrutiny of policy makers and the general public (Wheeler et. al., 2008). We see this in the documentation of The Spellings Commission Report (2006), which reiterates that, in fact, there will be a substantial increase in the roles and responsibilities of the regional accrediting bodies. The Council on Higher Education Accreditation (CHEA) and programmatic and regional accreditation associates will bring renewed reflection to the process of reviewing and improving the accreditation process – including the issues of assessment, transparency, and improvements within the standards and documentation (Ruben et al, 2008).

The accountability and transparency of colleges and universities has become part of the fabric of higher education and is likely to continue to be in the future. Creation of strategic plans can provide direction, goal achievement, and information to the institution, programs and other stakeholders.

Driving forces for the higher education business unit leaders in this study were found to be primarily internal factors of executive administration direction and the mission of the institution.

The external drivers to strategic planning, in contrast to the literature, were primarily market penetration and competition to remain a viable institution. The specialty accreditation of IACBE also played a motivational role in the business leader's strategic plan creation. Minimal motivation from the regional accrediting bodies was perceived to be seen globally by the institution and not the business units. This may be a direct result of accountability, where regional accreditation is only a driving force every 8-10 years upon accreditation renewal. Conversely, IACBE annual reports must reflect the current strategic plan to maintain accreditation of the business programs.

The Venn diagram in Figure 3 shows the overlapping internal and external driving forces working together. *P*, in the center of the diagram depicts the strategic plan. Areas I, II, and III motivate the leaders to create the strategic plan. Area I demonstrates the need for the leaders to give attention to external market factors, which is the primary driving force in this study. However, a SWOT analysis, (Strengths, weaknesses, opportunities, and threats) was the only environmental scanning used. Area II recommends that the participants understand and address both regional and specialty accrediting body's strategic planning requirements, Area III integrates both the internal and external environments and the understanding of how both influence the strategic planning efforts.

Internal Forces
Mission &
Administration

P In the center depicts the strategic plan with overlapping internal and external forces as motivation to the business leaders.

I: Depicts the need for administration to give attention to external market factors when creating a strategic plan
II: Recommendation of knowing accrediting body requirements when creating a strategic plan.
III: Understanding the FULL environment when creating a strategic plan.

Figure 3. Driving forces to strategic plan.

A limitation and requested enhancement of the strategic planning process is the involvement, understanding and input to the strategic plan by internal and external constituents. This would include all leaders, faculty, and staff with input from external constituents such as students, advisory boards and the community at large. Consistent with this phenomenon is the lack of transparency to the community where both internal publication and external information is not divulged.

If the findings from the Spellings Commission study that suggested planning are less than fully effective in higher education, strategic planning and the need for an educational model is definitely an area of improvement and easily rectified by the gathering of substantial data to obtain a model for higher education that will be both accountable and transparent to the public.

Section II: Process & Framework of a Strategic Plan

Few theorists question the function of strategic planning as a guide to the achievement of a vision, goals and objectives created by the institution. However, the development of strategic planning has produced in-depth, detailed, and cumbersome documents that are rarely flexible in a changing environment. Past attempts to connect strategic planning with higher education institutions has encountered differences in governance, structure, language, values, analytical demands, exceptions, spans of control, and decision making. These differences have contributed to an unhappy marriage between higher education and strategic planning (Dolence, 2004).

In the past, colleges and universities use various strategic planning paradigms resulting in a broad range of measured successes. Institutions have processes in place for budgets, strategies, and learning outcomes assessment but rarely integrate them in unified form. This lack of integration often leads to frustration throughout the organizations and stakeholders. More importantly, it may also result in suboptimal performance (Roller et al., 2004).

The research question addressing how the participants implement their strategic plans in their programs and integrated within their college/university is covered in this section. In addition, how the strategic plans created is addressed in this section. The need for a facilitator and a structure of the business unit's planning process addresses the manner in which business units plan.

Creation Process of Strategic Planning

The participants in this study were not given a strategic planning model; they were instead asked to interpret their process of creation. There were several additional questions that specifically addressed elements essential to the success of planning models within the literature.

The participants were asked to take the researcher step-by-step through their strategic plan creation process. In addition probing questions were asked of the participants to describe specific aspects of their plan. These questions were designed to (a) validate their knowledge of strategic plan creation and implementation, and (b) determine if that knowledge of strategic planning framework is implemented in their business unit.

Models used in higher education are based upon the models both in business and in academia, with the literature depicting several variations to these models. A simplified model of strategic planning in business and academics found previously in the literature review can be found in Figure 2. This model is taking the literature models and summarizing the results.

Each participant gave the impression they understood the elements of this type of strategic plan. This was consistent with the participants' education and experiential background in Chapter 4: Demographics. The participants were not given a particular model but, instead, were asked what elements were used in their planning. These individuals, as part of their education and curriculum and confidence found previously in this study, were assumed to have insight on structure and background knowledge in the field with a corporate-oriented discipline of strategic planning models. The administrative position held also implied that these individuals would have the understanding, insight and experience available to draw upon in this research to provide an increase insight and recognition of the evolving theory.

Organizational leaders understand and direct the vision of an institution that embodies the cultural beliefs, values and assumptions of its members (Schein, 1985). The leaders in a business program or college within the institution, as part of their education and curriculum, are assumed to have insight on structure and background. The exploration in this portion validates the evidence of participants' knowledge and compliance to their missions; goals (both in operations and curriculum); measurement of student learning outcomes assessment; and, finally, strategies and action plans for their business units.

Facilitator Discussions

As part of this confidence validation, the participants were asked their perspectives regarding facilitators and their help in the creation of a strategic plan. The participants did report a clear understanding of the strategic planning elements. In addition, they responded that their own knowledge was sufficient in creating strategic plans for their business units and could help to facilitate the creation process for other department and participate in the process for their institution. In addition, many of the participants indicated their faculty possessed this knowledge as well.

When asked if a facilitator was ever used or consulted to create their strategic plan; only one participant used or consulted a facilitator, however, the facilitator was used for the institutional, not the business unit plan. The majority of the participants responded that they personally possessed the expertise and the knowledge of strategic planning. Some even gave credit to the expertise of their faculty, reflected in these statements:

No, do it on my own. I have a couple of smart behavioral folks in my area, they are my counselors.

I think a management school faculty are used to strategic planning and do pretty well with my leadership.

No, I am a professional at that [strategic planning].

No we haven't [used a facilitator]. We use one of our faculty who is a trained facilitator.

We haven't no. Early in 2000 we did have a facilitator for the whole institution. I don't think a facilitator would do better than we do; I have a faculty member trained as a facilitator, we use him to facilitate ours, he knows our institution, and he does a good job.

A few participants commented on the consultation of the IACBE and other member institutions for help and guidance in the creation of their strategic plans.

I received enough assistance from IACBE, and local help that was plenty of support. I would say it would have been better, absolutely, if a facilitator was used.

We really got so much assistance form IACBE especially our friends at a local college; I would say that was our support system.

Two participants revealed that their institutional consultation had negative impact, and knowledge of the institution was a key factor, *"No, the last president tried that and it backfired. That person did not know our institution."* Similarly the negative experience was a facilitator that only listened to conflicts in the institution.

We [the institution] hired a consultant who met to vent only; [he] was not helpful. Initial review, we hired a consultant; we met twice in 9 months and vented history, personalities, direction, and managerial problems. Frankly, we just ended up using IACBE framework for the business area.

Several participants reported that a facilitator might be helpful as the facilitator would enter the institution with objectivity; however each one cited constraints of budget and resources needed to obtain a facilitator.

We don't use one, but I think they would be very helpful. They could remove themselves from the process and look at things more objectively; haven't got one because of budget.

No, probably would not be realistic because resources would not be available. We are totally dependent on tuition, and no endowments.

Facilitators can point out different things because they have a more objective point of view to the conversation. We do not use one here, probably because of budget.

I think in our school the faculty is used to this kind of thing, and they do pretty well with me leading. A facilitator could help for special projects, but there are budget constraints to that.

However, one participant pointed out an interesting perspective about bringing external data to the institution: Because one of the key factors of external forces was the market analysis, a facilitator could help in obtaining an environmental scan.

Personally I don't like to use one. We just talked and brainstorm; this is an internal document and my experience is that we just sit around and talk. This time around they actually had data, which is what the facilitator should bring to the table—market data and [he should] know competition.

The established institutional process is an important component of the business unit's strategic plan creation, as well as in the integration of the plan within the institution. Significant dialogue with the participants, focused on top- down or bottom-up models in their institution, assisted the researcher's understanding of the integration process. In the literature, this integration of the business and other departmental strategic planning with the overall institutional strategic plan is known as a bottom-up approach to strategic planning. This "grass roots," or bottom-up, approach to strategic planning has been accomplished with input from a variety of organizational constituents or units. Conversely the more traditional top-down planning is typically employed and directed by central office administrators and is influenced significantly by the culture of the institution (Rieger, 1994).

The bottom-up and top-down approaches, clarified in Roller et al. (2004), are important to this research topic. The top-down approach to planning is initialized by an administration that sets mission, goals and objectives. The bottom-up model allows the individual units to initiate and create strategic plans based on institutional mission and goals. The unit plan includes recommendations for budgets based on the propensity for carrying out the objectives and actions of the unit. This plan is then compiled for each area; the administration then decides upon the priority of objectives for each area, and the budget is then negotiated and reflects the priorities.

Interestingly, respondents were evenly divided between the two process models, i.e., a 50/50 split response for each process. However, neither model was a stand-out in any of the five types of institutions. Ten of the 20 participants reported that their model was top –down; the process was coordinated through the office of the Provost or Vice President of Academic Affairs and one institution coordinated through the president. Some respondents discussed the reasoning behind this type of model; it was either the preference of the administration or the structure of the institution, *"Yes, top-down, the president felt we should have a series of meetings over the campus, a draft, a framework, to have a general idea of where we were going as an institution."*

One participant responded top-down but believed the process may be a combination of both *"I don't think it will ever be completely top-down. It will be a combination. Top-down is more like values, not directives."*

The participating leaders cited different perspectives of why the process was driven from the top. One participant reported that it was due to the size and enrollment strategies of the institution. This participant stated,

> *Strategic planning comes heavily from the top because we are a very hierarchical organization and very large, and because we are an enrollment driven strategy and focus on enrollment counts, [we] bring in X amount of students, we in the business department must then plan for them.*

Another reason for allocating resources from the top was budget limitation and resource allocation. Through comparison for all top-down processes, it was consistently noted by the participants that the mission, goals and direction to the business units came from the top.

> *No, [the plan] is mostly top-down and budget related; allocation of resources is what drives the operational side.*

Every unit with budget responsibilities in the institution uses the initial plan and creates and implements a strategic plan for their unit. An important element of this type of approach is that the budget is set and may act as a limitation to the plan.

One participant also mentioned the specific accrediting body requirements, *"I would say that we are top-down. I think in most departments, the strategic plan is similar to mine depending on the specific requirements from their accrediting bodies in other schools."*

The other ten institutions identified a bottom-up strategic planning process. Even though the plan may not have been initiated by the administration, the business leader did show focused efforts in tying the mission, goals and directions to those of the institution. The participants used the directives from administration in the form of goals, initiatives, strategies, critical success factors, competencies, key performance indicators and other terminology as a starting point in the creation of their strategic plans.

I think it is iterative it starts with the institutional goals so we have a context in which to work. Clearly it flows up and, if accepted, becomes part of the institution's plan the following year.

Even though it is formulated at the top, really it is a bottom-up driven process. The functional units involve all their personnel, prepare the document and send it to the cabinet. Items are prioritized and funded accordingly. I think it is really bottom-up.

Definitely a bottom-up process. We had conference meetings, focus groups from all over the campus. We even talked about how many schools there should be on campus...very much bottom-up.

The participants did reveal some frustration, not with the formulation of their business unit plan in the bottom– up model, but in the integration of their plan by the administration. One participant stated, *"With a new VPAA on board, the plans will now be shared and integrated with all departments, a lot more with this administration, bottom-up, not sure if it is integrated now."*

Other comments include,

The plan is to pull all strategic plans together, but it hasn't happened yet. They [administration] gave us the charge, but when it got down to it for the college, and I can only speak for us, it was more bottom-up. The goals come from the institution administration, and

*our goals are set by the department. The assessment at the end is sent to administration,
bottom-up.*

*Another frustration was the inability of other departments to formulate their strategic plans.
I tend to conduct analysis, get feedback, set goals and then send it up to the VPAA, but I don't
have a lot of confidence it is integrated with other departments. The budget is the only process
that pulls together an institutional plan; we have some work to do there.*

One participant that was placed in the bottom-up category revealed that the business department
strategic plan was *isolated*, not used by administration and not really used by the department on a
consistent basis. One isolated comment was, "The strategic plan was only a document for
accreditation."

Framework for the Model Creation

After the participants established the structure of the institutional process they described the
plan's creation from initiation to completion to gain perspectives of framework.

Strategic plan models used in higher education are based upon the models uses in business and
described in the literature. Each participant was confident in describing his or her understanding of the
strategic plan creation framework, process and implementation. The researcher probed for
understanding through a series of questions regarding the strategic planning process.

In the literature, the first component was a connection to the institutional mission, vision and
goals. Consistent with traditional strategic planning models include the following elements: A SWOT
/STEP analysis, market analysis, program strategies, program objectives, outcomes measurements,
budget allocation to outcomes, implementation, and reporting. These can also be seen in the description
of terms in Chapter 1.

In reality, the participants may have an understanding of the strategic planning framework; but
not all used or implemented the elements from the literature search. An in depths look at all elements
the participants used successfully emerged from the interview data.

Participant responses revealed a number of these elements found in the literature models, which
met the criteria consistent with business industry strategic planning structure. All participants, when
discussing their initial responses with regards to the top-down or bottom-up structure of their

institutional process, validated a need to correlate the business unit plan to that of the institution. Probing produced a more complex picture.

The participants responded with a strong correlation to the mission and goals of the institution; those participants that followed the goals of the institution were very positive in their correlation efforts. The positive correlations were seen primarily in the top-down structures.

Goals meet the College and mission; we are very careful to tie back to the institution in whatever we do. We have a grasp on the process of assessment, set the goals and measure them and develop plans, assess, adjust and correct.

There is a direct correlation to the goals of the institution. That is the main concern when we are developing our SP. We are very careful to tie back to the institution.

There is direct correlation to the goals and mission of the institution.

Some followed the goals of their institutions, but made modifications when creating objectives and accountability for action plans. Two participants, from historically faith-based institutions, were using bottom-up models, and stressed that they received minimal direction from administration.

We use the College goals as a basis; we adopt our strategies and activities of the business unit to the goals of the college. I don't set up separate action plans, I set up different objectives, list the time table, person responsible, identify resources on n annual basis, and give a copy to the VPAA.

It is fair to say I create my own objectives off of the College goals. We have specific action plans that we gave piece by piece to the faculty members.

Another two responses were worth noting as they did not necessarily agree with or link their business unit goals to those of the institution. The remainder of the participants responded favorably regarding the linked to the mission and goals of the institution.

That is a tough one; we are sometimes at odds with the College for goals. We don't want to end up in the same place; do we get there? Probably.

We don't control enrollment management, we just have to adapt to the number coming in. We base our plan on historical data and have faculty ready; we have to be flexible and agile.

Essential Elements of Strategic Plans

When the participants described their "step-by-step" strategic planning process and the type of terminology used, the majority of the participants linked directly to the literature strategic planning models. Not all participants used a planning model, some were either a modified model from their education and/or business experience, or they followed the model set forth by the institution or IACBE. A few remaining leaders did not follow a conventional model. Participants discussed the framework of strategic planning as they affirmed the elements used within their perspective plan creation.

During this data analysis, ordering the elements from the participant's responses was consistent to the literature model. Although grounded theory is not designed to verify the models in literature, it was important to first inquire what elements are used by the participants. The degree to which elements were implemented and the degree to which they were modified and implemented varied based on the perspective of the participants. The participants identified essential elements that did become part of the grounded theory model.

The majority of the participants began with their outcomes assessment from the prior year and a current SWOT analysis. Participants responded that the process included a gathering or "retreat" of business unit personnel to obtain pertinent information and obtain buy-in. They had this to say:

Our process is ongoing; we accumulate those results [outcome assessment] and use them in our annual retreat. We also discuss the SWOT analysis from the year before and discussed what has changed for our organization. We brainstorm, look at opportunities, prioritize the items and rank the action plans. The action plans are assigned responsibility, or subcommittees are assigned to a particular task.

We start with an annual review of outcomes assessment and prior year goals from administration; we then brainstorm, evaluate SWOT every other year, develop strategies, and discuss new programming and funding required. We also assess program: size, enrollments, input with curricular review that includes outcomes assessment.

We start with gathering outcomes assessment information and SWOT for our program, every year other program [unit] does the same. We meet with the entire college for a planning day and obtain high level Success Factors and Goals from administration, the business program retreats, review curriculum, prioritize objectives (curricular and operational) and action plans, decide on measurements, assign responsibility.

We started three years ago with a bottom-up approach, SWOT, Market analysis, faculty participation, to executive team review broad stroke items. All other departments then participated, board of directors gave initial approval, review with faculty to develop, budget, finance, enrollment and, come up with action plans, six year plan, work in progress, reviewed annually.

In Section I, a major driver, regardless of category, was *market focus* with a need to remain competitive in that market. Only one participant mentioned a market analysis in his unit's process. All processes did not include a specific market analysis, only a SWOT in which the opportunities and threats are viewed from external data. One participant addressed this issue,

There is really not a market analysis; there is a SWOT analysis that gets put into the competitive forces, but not a lot on that. More emphasis is placed on objectives and detailed tactical plans to achieve objectives. I assign people, but it falls on me to gather that information.

Another said,

Outcomes assessment and enrollment data are reviewed at a retreat for the business program and division. We also do a market analysis as part of the annual report to IACBE. We finalize our budget based on this for next academic year.

One participant made a suggestion to assist stakeholders in understanding the terminology.

I put a glossary of terms at the end of my strategic plan. We plan for enrollment numbers and financial viability. We have measurable objectives and strategies to accomplish them. Each strategy has an action plan and budget implications. We are trying to tie in assessment, each objective, and learning or operational is assessed.

The participants above started the process with previous year measurements, reviewed their SWOT analysis, created goals, objectives and action plans. These actions were consistent with literature recommendations. Other responses were brief; however, they followed the same pattern in the overarching process.

We start as a department in September and October gathering our outcome assessment results by looking at the outcome of our measurement tools and discuss if we did we meet our goals. We then make directional changes, adjust the plan, written form is provided to everyone and IACBE.

We do a SWOT analysis every year as part of an annual report in June. Specify the results of the goals we had the previous years and review performance. We assign responsibilities; the annual report is a bit more tactical than strategic.

Some participants gave very brief descriptions and mentioned only a few of the elements in their strategic plans; some elements were even modified or omitted.

I don't set up separate action plans, I set up different objectives, list the time table, person responsible, identify resources on an annual basis, and give a copy to the VPAA.

We create a formal plan. We look at SWOT, and we look at the market analysis regularly because we "pull" for the students. There is a huge amount of marketing, and we also have action plans.

Yes we have measureable objectives. We don't use a specific model for our strategic plan, when I got to the operational effectiveness plan, I did use a model that a different school used at one of the IACBE conferences; they were talking about operational effectiveness.

Everyone that reports to the president has an action plan; my division chair and faculty submit action plans to me.

A number of the leaders had taken on the responsibility of writing the strategic plan themselves. My area has several improvements, the action plans are assigned to the program director, and we are accountable for our own goals. I will ask for volunteers, or I will do them myself. We are currently in the process of creating more action plans.

Honestly, I wrote the first draft, my supervisor edited it, and I shared it with my department. It [strategic plan] had traditional structure, goals, objectives and action plans we did a SWOT analysis as well.

We have a very raw plan, and I lead that initiative in the department. We prioritize and rank the actions plans. We try to invite others in the institution to get their input. Our action plans are primarily for one year and there are assigned responsibilities and constant updates.

Honestly, when it comes to the strategic plan of the department, I talk with my faculty and take their ideas and put them in a plan. I try to relieve as much administrative burden from the faculty as I can so they can focus on teaching.

Three participants responded with specific modifications to their planning process. The following modifications to the plans illustrate the challenges with outcomes assessment and budget integration; they are viewed (in these responses) as separate entities, apart from the strategic plan.

Our operational plans are separate from the outcomes assessment plans. I do it, I talk with faculty get their ideas and put them into a plan. I take it back and discuss it with them regarding the outcomes assessment results, professional growth, and active engagement. Also included are, long term stakeholder relations, current technology, recruitment goals, and diverse population.

The budget is a separate priority, and not tied to the strategic plan.

Everyone that reports to the president has an action plan. My division chair and faculty submit action plans to me. Outcomes assessment is a separate process.

Surprising to the researcher, there were leaders who were not as confident of their process as their education and experience would suggest. The data revealed that either the participants (a) were not sure of their process, (b) knew what to do but did not implement, or (c) the plan is not a priority to the institution. The responses below illustrate this phenomenon and were from bottom-up institutional processes with minimal intervention from administration.

I can't remember what step [element] came first. One other person in our department knows how to do it [strategic planning], so we did it ourselves.

I don't think we really do action plans. We have drifted away from the original document and I have not gone back to read it. We look at our curriculum and what we are teaching through outcomes.

No one really monitors our strategic plan We self-monitor and report annually, then put into place new action plans for the gaps that are identified and new items to be included: goals, objectives, and action plans.

We do have operational goals, but not really operational like an industrial perspective. What operational functions do faculty have? The chair has the responsibility to make sure it integrates and dove tails into the larger institution, so the plan is not operational in the commercial operational sense.

The remainder of similar responses was from top-down administrative initiatives. The data revealed that participants perceived pressure from the administration to implement action plans.

Getting the students into the prerequisite classes to the MBA program at the institution, all resources are tied to these.

That is a tough one; we are sometimes at odds with the College for goals. We don't want to end up in the same place. An example would be getting more students in than we can handle or keeping our standards of the business area.

We base the plan on enrollment directives from administration and rely on our reputation with alumni. So, we don't have to devote a lot of energy to break out our strategies for growth.

Operationally, I don't think we really do action plans. We have drifted away from the original document, and I have not gone back to read it. We look at our curriculum and what we are teaching through outcomes.

Review and Implementation of the Strategic Plans

After the plan is created, either "top-down" or "bottom-up," how are the strategic plans implemented in their units and integrated within their institution? Data revealed that strategic planning was completed for a term longer than a year, such as a 3-5 year basis. The strategic plan review was completed primarily on an annual basis and the majority of participants followed their academic calendars in contrast to having an annual or fiscal calendar. Some action plans and larger projects planning were set outside of the annual timeframe.

The implementation phase mainly followed the initiatives of the administration with varying degrees of accountability. This was a frustration for the business leader, and it is a challenge to implement or integrate a strategic plan within their programs with difficulty in obtaining buy-in from the faculty. Participants also responded that other departments within the institution did not complete a separate strategic plan like the business unit and were not held accountable.

The researcher obtained information about the frequency of review and implementation for their created plans. The majority of participants reported the structure was clear and easily followed and reviewed on an annual basis. Some of these responses are seen below;

We came up with a document that represents our action plans going forward, we redo our action plan each year, but we don't make it a one year plan, because some of the plans take more than one year, so we keep them in the document and show progress. We don't have it set at five years, it may be shorter, but the larger goals are extended.

We start from the general institutional plan consisting of published annual goals and objectives sheet which is an annual revision to a five year strategic plan.

Some action plans are longer than a year, but the plan is flexible and we review it each year.

Some participants, where they are aware of their review process, reported that work on the strategic plan was on-going, *"We have a six year plan, that is still being tweaked, and they are still coming up with things to do, and we are still setting priorities. It is a work in progress, never totally finished."*

One participant expressed frustration with the formal document and the "irritation" of annual review,

I am sure that there is a formal document, but I don't think that anyone thinks about it on a daily basis or pulls it out and says are we doing our strategic plan. Certainly, we have a review process every year and to be honest we view it as an irritation.

Another participant did not have the ability to update their plan on annual basis, it was a five year plan and revised on the administrative level,

Basically, we have a five year plan, it is disseminated, bound and handed to the departments and available on our Web, but the details of how they revise it usually happens through the president, VPAA and senior team.

A third participant articulated his feelings regarding a need for a more systematic review. Other participants, whose plans were more than one year in duration, agreed.

Actually, it [strategic plan] is an operational plan with bigger goals extending 3-5 years in the future. Most of it is a one year operational focus. In a year, we would like to be more strategic, but we are so tuition driven, and our enrollment fluxes from year to year. We probably don't review systematically, but not at certain intervals. There is probably a flaw in that.

Limitations and Enhancements of Essential Elements

1. **Simplification of the plan:** Only two participants in the study expressed the complexity of the institutional plan as a limitation to the process. The participants had this to say,

   One thing I would say is that our planning document is huge and hard to get your arms around it because it covers so many areas. I wish we could have more of a abbreviated document that the average employee could look at and see what the strategic direction was. At some level, you need the detail, but the average person does not need all of the detail to see what the direction is.

   I think the challenges are going to be the same for most institutions. Organizations must remain more and more fluid, ready to change and remain flexible. The changes we have done over the past years have helped us to address that. In particular I think of the strategic planning and the importance of accreditation in higher educational institutions.

The need to simplify the document to make it readable and flexible is an important enhancement to this limitation. Participants expressed the need for to enhance the essential elements and streamline data gathering. As an enhancement, the following leaders wanted to focus on the simplification of data collection in their strategic plans.

I would like to simplify . . . the accumulation and analysis of all the measurements we make. It is time-consuming. I tend to blow them off sometimes. If there was a way we could streamline the collection and analysis of data that would be more fun.

I would probably kill the data piece, the data feedback loop. I would like to find ways to simplify the metrics I need to keep an eye on to make sure we are efficient and effective.

2. *Prioritization*: This was the second enhancement to the essential functions of the plan.

This did link to the need for administration to communicate the focus and priority of strategies as it flowed down to the units in a top-down structure. Conversely, in the bottom-up process, the leaders must understand priorities of the institution through institutional goals for direction in strategy creation. Participants expressed the need for simplification and streamlining of the essential elements and the accumulation of data.

I think I would narrow it down somewhat, so that you don't get too much stuff in it. Sometimes we get so fragmented, trying to measure to many things and do to many things, we can't do it all. We currently don't prioritize, we should.

Units of the institution needed to develop goals that were compatible with institutional initiatives, thus, a higher level focus was needed to help prioritize and allocate resources to the strategies:

With a shorter list of strategies and plans plus prioritizing at the end of the process would be better. Getting more integration with central administration would definitely be helping the process, so when we go for budget money they would understand where we are, and possibly fund more.

I think we could take it up one level, so instead of having so much detail I think we could actually do it at a larger view. We tried so hard to closely correlate every single goal we had and identify objectives and action plans for every single one. Our goals are fairly broad based, so we felt in order to cover them we ended up creating all this stuff.

3. *Integration* of the strategic plan into the institutional plan was found to be the third limitation. This phenomenon was not seen as much in the top-down model because it initially is driven by administration. The top-down approach gives a clearer understanding of the institution's mission and goals. Integration can take on so many meanings. In this review of integration limitation, the researcher found that the meaning of integration may translate to the integration of resources commitment, which is seen in this response:

There is a lack of integration and a lot of good ideas without resource commitment to make it happen. I think that is major problem inherent in the planning process always and that is managing expectations. A lot of people get energized by the planning process, and they get to the point of looking at the resources allocated to them, and there is such a huge gap in their dreams and the reality of resources that people just give up. This makes it even harder to get them engaged in the next phase of the planning process.

Even the top-down models had issues with resource allocation.

The only limitation to the plan that I see is that we have an institutional model and we have input from all of the departments on environmental scanning and outcomes, we really don't have individual plans in the departments, only an institutional plan, so you are vying for your agenda and allocation of limited resources.

Integration of institutional initiatives was part of not only integration of individual plans but also includes the outcomes assessment and what is need both from the academic side and the operational units.

To us it would be more useful when we do our strategic plan and especially development of our strategies we feel are necessary, to have a little bit of an opportunity to see if there is any interest of those strategies from the top so that we might see if there are any resources we might have to follow the strategies downward.

The challenge for me is, I can do this in the department, we have our outcomes assessment, and we have our strategic plans, and I try to budget accordingly. But until the institution as a whole is serious about linking the assessment to strategic planning and budgeting, I can create all the

plans I want, but I don't know how to say this, but until that process of linking takes place at a
higher level, it is just paperwork.

Enhancements of the *integration* phenomenon were also discussed by participants. The suggestions for better integration mirrored the limitations in the integration of budget, environmental scanning, focused strategy and assessment. These issues are expressed by:

Work on the integration of budget and the planning process, also more frequent reporting.

We are so large that we need more multidirectional input from the top to get the goals and up to the top with environmental information from the advisory boards.

One participant made an observation regarding the flexibility of the plan. New initiatives during implementation are more difficult to integrate if the plan is static.

Another thing is that we just launched another initiative that is not in the strategic plan this year and it is hard to integrate new ideas if the plan is static. I would like to find a way to integrate new ideas.

Finally, this comment was made from a participant using a bottom-up structure with the issue of integration of other department reports,

I would like to have someone at the institutional level who has a better understanding of how to effectively integrate planning, budget and assessment over all of the academic units to facilitate the integration into the institutional strategic plan.

Summary of Section II Process and Framework of Strategic Planning

The emergent elements of the process appeared to be consistent across all types of institutions and coincide with the literature. Although some participants may not have perceived the same elements, a pattern was not found specific to any type of institution.

The majority of participants reported no need of a facilitator in the creation of their strategic plans. Budget constraints and lack of institutional knowledge were common responses against the use of a facilitator. Not requiring a facilitator did reflect the self-evaluation of *confidence* by the participants.

The structure of the institutional strategic planning process did play a much bigger role in the perspectives of the participants. Linking the organization's strategic plan and the departmental strategic plan can be challenging either in a bottom-up approach or top-down approach. Consensus was that a clear understanding and easily integrated organizational mission and goals was required. In addition, there was consensus that all institutional departments should develop goals compatible with institutional goals. Interestingly, participants reported a 50/50 split for each process.

The bottom-up model required the individual units to initiate and create a strategic plan based on the mission and goals of the institution. The unit plans included recommendations for budgets based on their ability to carry out the objectives and actions of the unit. This bottom up model reflected the *lack of integration* by administration and *incomplete strategic plans by other departments* in the institution.

Half of the 20 participants responded that their model was "top –down", i.e., for ten sites, the process was coordinated through the office of the Provost or Vice President of Academic Affairs; and one institution coordinated through the President. These participant responses were more positive in nature and the participants responded with a strong *connection to the mission and goals* of the institution requiring more *accountability* for the action plans in their strategic plan.

The *lack of integration* of strategies, budget allocation and assessment are seen as limitations to both structures. Enhancements can be made with multidirectional communication and prioritization and focus by administration.

In constructing the strategic plan, again, the entire group of participants in this study expressed strong *confidence* in their education and especially in their business experience. The leaders are assumed to have insight on structure and background knowledge in the field with a corporate-oriented discipline of strategic planning models. This coincides with the statement from Seagren et al., (1994), who stated, there has been a growing need to recast the academic leader as a business officer first who understands and encourages faculty development and growth.

With this knowledge, the participants used models primarily from the business industry with significant modifications for integration into the educational strategic planning. The other model used frequently was the Integrated Model from IACBE found in Figure 1. With constant comparison analysis, the emergent educational strategic plan framework produced *essential elements of a strategic plan*, formal and informal.

The participants began with a SWOT analysis or review of student learning outcomes. The analysis of the data found discrepancies in the use of outcomes assessment measurements. It was previously assumed through the IACBE model, that outcomes assessment would be a learning goal or objective within the strategic plan. Interestingly enough, a model in academia is not found that truly integrates outcomes assessment globally for all institutions.

All participants did give an affirmation of measuring student learning outcomes, or using the results for planning. However, data revealed that not all interviewees were comfortable with student learning outcomes but were aware of requirements by the IACBE. The majority used outcomes assessment as part of their department practice but most participants perceived that the outcomes assessment was not easily incorporated into the strategic planning process. The underlying variable that prevented integration was similar to the "bottom-up" structure where not all departments in the institution were required to measure and monitor student learning outcomes. The outcomes assessment in this study were, for the majority of participants was primarily a different plan or document that was measured separately and used as input to the review of student learning outcomes.

When researching external forces that drive the creation of strategic plans, strong opinions of market penetration as the number one external force were given. However, as shown above, only student learning outcomes and external opportunities and threats of the SWOT analysis were reviewed. There was no inclusion of an environmental STEP analysis and only two participants had completed an external market analysis. One participant gave an idea for facilitator use, as they would be external consultants helpful in gathering and disseminating objective information for the business units, "Personally I don't like to use one [facilitator]…they actually had data, which is what the facilitator should bring to the table market data and know the competition."

In addition to the SWOT analysis and minimal external market information that were identified as the largest driving forces for the business units, leaders also agreed that setting goals and objectives drove their plans. Most participants revealed the difficulty in the creation of clear objectives and action plans when the budget limitations and administrative directives were not clear.

The framework questioning revealed a simplified list of seven *essential elements* used or perceived important in the creation of strategic plans by the participants.

1. Mission & Institutional Goals
2. Environmental Scanning
   a. SWOT analysis
   b. Market analysis (shown need, rarely completed)
   c. Student Learning Outcomes Data

3. Strategy Formulation
   a. Goals (some correlated to the institution goals)
   b. Objectives: student learning and operational
4. Implementation - Action plans
6. Assessment – measurement tools
7. Budget Integration

The literature review, Figure 4 and Figure 5, provided a basic strategic planning model for the business and educational areas for both top-down and bottom-up structures. In addition, the integrated strategic plan model provided to the members of IACBE is very similar to the business industry models. However, in this study, the reality of model use and perceptions of the participants, through inductive reasoning, allowed the researcher to develop a model of academic strategic planning found in Chapter 6.

The top-down structure, followed by 50% of the participants, followed the flow of the *essential elements*, but exhibited substantial differences from the top-down model described in the literature. The primary driving force, (A) market analysis, was not completed in the majority of the business units nor within their institutions. In addition very little information by external stakeholders was obtained. The implementation of the strategic plans revealed that only (B) action plans were created without integration to the budget process and (C) student learning outcomes were an isolated plan, primarily in the business unit and not always used in the environmental scanning. These measurements are covered in Section III of this chapter.

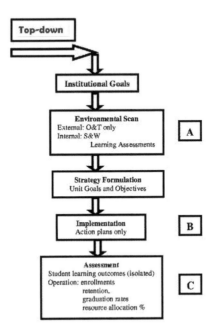

Figure 4. Top-down differences to literature.

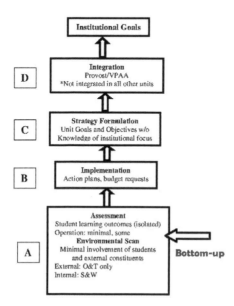

Figure 5. Bottom-up differences to literature.

The bottom-up model emergent from the participants is seen in Figure 5.

Participants began the process with (A) the SWOT analysis, which was isolated to the business units with little input from outside stakeholders; a market analysis was not completed by the business units. The participants responded that even though the personnel in their departments were asked to participate in this annual process, there was very little buy-in. Student learning outcomes and operational measurement data is used to create future objectives and action plans.

In the next step, (B) business unit leaders completed strategic planning annually with objectives, action plans and budget requests based on the environmental scanning and assessment data. The plan is sent to the Provost/VPAA for integration. All business unit leaders reviewed their strategic plans at least annually but rarely reported their progress to institutional administration. Reporting was primarily internal within the department addressing strategic planning limitations to the unit participants.

The next step, (C), represents important factors in strategy formation using the mission and direction of the institutional administration. This was not done on a consistent basis; the majority of the participants completed their plans without input from the institutional administration. However, all participant's correlated their objectives to the mission and goals of the institution.

Finally step (D) represents integration. In this study, ten business unit participants created goals and objectives without direction from institutional administration revealed in step C. The participants reported that a number of other departments/programs in the institution did not provide goals, objectives, action plans and budget requests on a consistent basis; this is shown by the dashed-line arrow to the integration of their plan to the institutional. Some participants reported that their plan was isolated and they were not aware of other department resources allocation. The participants indicated a lack of integration by the Provost/VPAA and the lack of integration with other departments.

Section III: Achievement of Successful Strategic Plans

Goals are the broader statements of intent, whereas, objectives, long term or annual, should be measurable, quantitative, challenging, realistic, consistent, and prioritized (David, 2007). It is assumed that goal statements of the business unit are linked to the institutional mission and goals. In a number of responses this was a true statement, more so in the top-down model driven by administration, but not as clear with the bottom-up model.

Participants responded that they used both student learning objectives and operational objectives in the creation of their strategic plans. They perceived them to be particularly important in the creation and direction of action plans and accountability measurements for those individuals assigned to the action plans.

Even though measurement tools for the objectives varied in use, they were required to demonstrate realized outcomes and success of objectives. These measurement tools contributed to the framework of a complete grounded theory model.

Measurement Tools

Measurement tools are used to obtain established objectives and ultimately the goals established for the institution. These participants, based on their *confidence* in the creation of their strategic plans, were assumed to be aware of the importance of objective measurements in achievement of their established goals.

As part of the strategic plan framework the researcher wanted to explore how the leader's goals and objectives were measured and how successful completion was perceived by the participants. Again, as in the structural framework of the strategic plan, factors for higher educational measurements of success began to emerge when the participants were asked to explain their strategic plan measurement tools both student learning and operational outcomes. These measurement tools were not found to differ in the type of IACBE institution. The measurement tool for student learning outcomes and operational objectives is shown separately.

Student Learning Outcomes Assessment

One measurable component is the student learning outcomes (or outcomes assessment); this continues to be a focus of the regional and specialty accrediting bodies. The integration of outcomes assessment in strategic planning continues to be difficult for most business units and institutions; this study affirmed that challenge. Many of the participants, especially in the bottom-up structure used student learning outcomes as isolated plans, not tied to strategic planning.

In January 2008, the Association of American Colleges and Universities (AACU) and the Council for Higher Education Accreditation (CHEA) issued "Principles for Student Learning and Accountability" as a framework for accountability and to help higher education institutions assess their contributions. The "principles" approach places primary responsibility on colleges and universities themselves for achieving excellence and assuring appropriate public accountability. That responsibility includes establishing and clearly stating their own goals; gathering evidence about how well student achieve these goals; communicating clearly their mission, goals, and effectiveness; carefully monitoring the use of federal funds; and emphasizing high standards, transparency, and accountability (Ruben et al., 2008).

This statement of accountability is again an essential element in the strategic planning process. The student learning outcomes have been a large part of regional accreditation since the late 1990's. Institutions have been given ample time to create measures, assess and drive student learning by a formal process within their institutions. With the assumption that student learning outcomes or outcomes assessment, is incorporated as part of the business strategic plan as required by the IACBE. Participants were asked how they accomplish this integration into their strategic plans.

As expected, all participants did give an affirmation of measuring student learning outcomes, and the majority of the participants are using the result for planning. All participants measured student learning outcomes and were aware of requirements by the IACBE, however they did state it was a constant work in progress.

The majority used outcomes assessment as part of their department practice but most participants perceived that the outcomes assessment was not easily incorporated into the strategic planning process.

The IACBE model was introduced in chapter 2 and is reproduced here for discussion purposes. Outcomes assessment is a learning goal or objective within the strategic plan. Interestingly enough, the researcher did not find any other models in literature that integrate outcomes assessment for academic programs and/or institutions. The underlying integration difficulty reported by the participants was that not all departments measure student learning outcomes; thus, in a bottom-up model, the business unit outcomes are the only outcomes available to institutional administration.

IACBE requires student learning outcomes assessment for specialty accreditation and the literature model demonstrated the integration of student learning outcomes into the business unit's strategic plan. This model illustrates outcomes assessment as part of the strategy evaluation with direct and indirect measurement for validation of student learning.

The participants' responses to an inquiry about outcomes assessment integration revealed that student learning outcomes were measured in the business unit as part of the IACBE requirement; however, there was minimal integration within the institutional strategic plan.

The participants that did integrate student learning outcomes also had an institutional strategic plan already established with student learning outcomes as the foundation. These processes were primarily in the top-down institutional structure.

Outcomes assessment is institutionally driven; every outcome is mapped to a course and to a syllabus. Yes we incorporate our outcomes assessment; it drives what you do in your programs.

I will tell you that our student learning outcomes are really what drive our organization and what I do in the academic level. As an institution, we follow more of a business model when it comes to strategic plans. But, as far as what drives our academic division, it is definitely the student learning outcomes.

In a top-down model, when the goals and objectives were dictated to the participants and faculty from institutional administration, some participants still struggled with objectives, action plans and the measurement of their success,

That is interesting questions...yes and no. I can tell you that everyone from the head of our division who reports to the President of our institution has objectives and action plans. I was laughing because the faculty struggle with what that action plan really is. In theory, you can map it to and institutional goal. We don't have a formal process of mapping like we do in student learning outcomes.

The following response illustrates one participant's isolation of the outcome assessment plans within their business units.

We have outcome assessment goals as part of learning and operational goals within our business department, not sure if other departments are similar?

One participant commented that the regional accreditation in addition to IACBE was cited as a motivational factor for outcomes assessment,

As an institution, we are in better shape at measuring student learning outcomes than we are at creation of a comprehensive institutional strategic plan. Outcomes assessment is largely driven by our regional accrediting body, Middle States, and it is an expectation for the whole organization. We address our outcome assessment issues as part of our action plans.

An unexpected finding occurred. Three participants centered their strategic plans only student learning outcomes. Each based the unit's "strategic plan" entirely on outcomes assessment of the business unit. Strategic planning of the outcomes assessment also included the operational objectives focused on student learning outcomes and how they are supported.

We had outcomes defined and then made action plans to meet the outcomes; that is how the strategic plan got started. Yes [outcomes assessment] integrated painfully. It was our starting point; I'm not sure if that is exactly the way to do it, but that was our starting point.

We do have outcomes assessment and departmental operating objectives that we follow in our strategic plan. We measure retention, recruitment, and student satisfaction measurements within the outcomes assessment.

Every competency has an assignment in class for outcomes assessment and we assess how that assignment met that competency; so, yes to your question, we strategically plan our assessment.
Student learning outcomes have been a part of the fabric of higher education since the late 1990s and are required by IACBE. Participants indicated that they continue to struggle, not only with the student learning outcomes measurements, but with the integration into the strategic plan of the unit. Unmistakably, these participants knew the requirements of outcomes; in reality, the integration of those outcome measurements into the strategic planning process have been disjointed and hard to incorporate into the process. This phenomenon cut across all types of institutions and was a problem for the majority of participants.

Actually, the process has been very disjointed in the past. Honestly, we've done outcomes assessment to meet our IACBE expectations and our NCA expectations, but there was no other correlation between outcomes assessment, strategic planning and budgeting.

As you know, leadership is not there yet; it has to come from the top and it is not there yet. But, as we move forward those links between outcomes and strategic planning will happen.

We are like a teenager in the growing up years. It is a stretch for a lot of us, integrating outcomes assessment into the strategic plan, and hopefully we will get through that transition.
Several participants voiced concerns with their outcomes assessment measurements.

Outcomes are not as strong as they need to be. That is one of our weaknesses in our strategic plan, for IACBE as well. We have some direct measures, but not as many as we really need and not as specific as they need to be. The primary learning outcomes I cannot document those with much confidence.

Outcomes assessment is not as strong as it needs to be; that is one of our weaknesses. It is hard to get collective buy-in from the faculty. We do well at indirect measurements such as surveys but, direct outcome measurements are weak for us.

We talk about outcomes assessment measurements but still struggle with them.

Operational Objectives

The objective of outcomes measurements is to review the results of an institution's or unit's operations (both academic and nonacademic) and determine if the objectives were realized (Roller et al., 2004). Some participants revealed an informal outcomes assessment plan for the IACBE with a primary focus on operational planning.

In terms of outcomes, that is not what the plan is talking about right now, it is operational...my issue is to hire faculty. As far as outcomes assessment, we are horribly lacking and we finally hired someone who helped save another school who is just as lacking as we are. So, we are working on it getting ready for MS, the major issues for our institution is infrastructure right now.

Outcomes assessment is really more of an appendix; but we do have specific action plans with people accountable.

We measure mostly our outcomes assessment for IACBE, not for the strategic plan.

Assessment measurements should include examining the operational results of the functional units of an institution. The support units of the institution should be aware of the learning outcomes and necessary strategies and how they can assist in the student's learning. There were a number of operational measurements that emerged from the data, among the highest occurrences were: enrollments, credit hours, retention, financial viability, graduation rates, and surveys from alumni, student satisfaction, and employers. Some surveys were part of the outcomes assessment process; some were not.

These participants used other operational measurements to obtain budget dollars.

We look at retention rates, outcome assessment measurements, pass rates for specific programs, student surveys, graduate surveys, faculty evaluations, on-line faculty evaluations, benchmarked with other institution's enrollments, credit hour generation and of course budget variances from the previous year.

We look at retention rate as the student moves through the programs and monitor this rate for success . . . this is hard because faculty control the content, and really, administrators don't really have much input of what is taught in the classroom.

One participant specifically reviewed size, enrollments and the amount of resources used. He stated,

Annually we take a look at our programs, the size, enrollments, inputs from the curricular view process and the results of our outcomes assessment. A big driver for the unit is looking at the amount of resources we have and how they are being used.

The more traditional operational measurements are seen in this set of responses as outlined in the framework of a strategic plan,

Operational measurements include enrollment, financial viability, measureable objectives and strategies to accomplish them. Each strategy has an action plan and budget implications. We are trying to tie in assessment, each objective, and learning or operational is assessed.

Yes, we did have operational measurements; but I will struggle to remember. Retention certainly. We look at jobs and salaries the students obtain. We do student and alumni surveys.

We align previous year's objectives; we try to quantify our objectives. For example, we are tuition-driven, so we look for expected enrollment goals.

Some were focused on growth including the allocation of resources as a measurement of success.

We have a specific goal related to productivity and growth with a percentage of institutional credit hours at 7% higher. So, as we grow, we monitor that the business department holds our own in terms of credit hours. I receive that data from the accounting office, and I make sure

93

that the amount of business we are doing as part of the institution is commiserate with our resources.

Cost versus expense is identified, for example equip all classrooms with technology, how much was spent. Beyond that, we really don't have any measurements.

Some participants had no measurable goals; however, lack of measurable goals did not seem to hinder the perceived achievement of an objective.

We really don't know when our goals are completed. Mainly we get together and review the assessment tools and see if we have achieved them; no major celebration.

Measurement is mainly by consensus that it is successful. We accomplished that, to achieve that action is pretty clear, the new curriculum, done, and out on the Web.

Yes, mainly by consensus that it is successful. Mostly through observation, if the document is there or if something is completed.

Summary of Section III: Achievement of Successful Strategic Plans

This section demonstrated the use of both student learning outcomes and operational measurements as part of the collection of data to be used for feedback into the strategic plan. This feedback is then used to make changes or suggest strategy improvements in the strategic plan.

Student learning outcomes have been a large part of regional accreditation since the late 1990's. Institutions have been given ample time to create measures, assess and drive student learning through a formal process. The data demonstrated that participants, business leaders in their initiations, perceived a disconnect between the outcomes assessment measures integration and the overall strategic plan. The participants revealed that they are measuring outcomes from a different plan, sometimes isolated, within their units. However, for the majority of participants, these results were evaluated along with the SWOT analysis prior to the establishment of goals and objectives for the unit.

The primary measurement tools were found to be:

1) Outcomes assessment; two direct, two indirect

2) Operational assessment
   a. Enrollments
   b. Retention
   c. Grad rates
   d. Resource allocation
   e. Surveys
       i.   Alumni
       ii. Student Satisfaction
       iii. Employer

These measurement tools, according to the participants, need to be simple, quantifiable and easily interpreted. The accumulation of data and lengthy analysis may endanger the completion or focus of the plan. One participant was adamant, "I would like to find ways to simplify the metrics and key on the data I need to keep an eye on to make sure we are efficient and effective."

Section IV: Budget Integration & Resource Allocation

Two components of a strategic plan, the budgeting process and allocation of resources, are areas of limited integration. In most cases, there are separate plans generated by the poorly-integrated processes (Roller et al., 2004). Most participants perceived that they were given adequate funding for their programs. However, the 50% of participants using a bottom-up structure expressed concern about funding priorities from institutional administration. Priorities included requirements to obtain adequate staffing, technology, supplies and other resources.

Participants primarily responded to the need for the strategic plans to drive the resource allocations. They identified student learning and operational objective cost allocation. The following four responses reflect this as an important component of the grounded theory model strategic plan. These participants were from top-down structures in their respective institutions.

I would definitely not receive the budget dollars, if I did not have a strategic plan. It is critical for us to demonstrate the need for resources and justify those resources based upon all measurements. So, strategic planning is the foundation to obtaining budget resources, specifically funding.

We make generalizations, prioritize resource allocation and funding. The only way to get extra resources is to take some away from someone else on campus.

The first year that we integrated the budget and strategic plan our budget increased because of our direct correlation between deliverables and clearly identifiable objectives and the dollars associated with them. We told the academic dean, "If we can't get the funding, which ones should be taken out?" Our budget was definitely affected and actually tripled.

The strategic plan is critical for us to demonstrate the need for resources. We justify those resources based upon our operational effectiveness measures, based on student learning outcomes, survey of students to find our weaknesses etc. Thus, that strategic planning is the foundation to obtain budget resources, especially new funding.

The remaining 16 participant responses, emergent across all IACBE institution types, addressed non- integration of the budget and strategic planning process. This process is driven by the revenue not directly by the plan. One participant reported, *"Our budget is driven by enrollments so, if we want a percentage increase in our enrollment, how much revenue do we get and what should we do with those dollars. That is why the strategic plan is so important for us."*

These participants did view the budget as prioritized by the administration with the organization's focus in mind integrated with the strategic plan, not necessarily the business unit. The budget was allocated without the business unit's input and was formulated by administration.

I would say that the strategic plan is created from the executive team who drive the budget and plan. The budgets will be allocated for the good of the organization and not necessarily for the good of the business unit. In that sense, it is really top-down; the strategic plan does drive our budget.

When we set our plan, we send our proposals forward; we have to include budget consequences. If we didn't show budget impact, I don't think we would get the same funding. But, we have been successful over the past couple of years using the accreditation process to increase the size of the faculty and increase our budget.

I would say budget plays a part, to some extent. Our institutional budget process could be improved. Ideally, you have a budget that rolls up information from your strategic plan and really drives, almost having a zero based budget each year. We really don't do that.

I am not aware of anyone except the business unit that has a strategic plan on campus. I don't think there is a great deal of push to tie strategic plans to the budget.

The following responses were induced by the researcher to have a top-down directive from administration, with little buy-in from the constituencies. Some participants articulated,

It is a strange budgeting process; not one that a person who has been in business would recognize. It is not related to the unit's strategic plan in any sense that I can see.

No, there is not a great deal of push there. Many times there are initiatives put into place, and I am not sure where those resources came from or that they were available; we don't link that closely. It is easy to put the mission statement together, but I always tell people, "Watch where the money goes, where the money goes, is where we focus many times." I do input each year into the process. I sit and show my projected needs, short term and long term.

No direct budget allocation, but that may change with the new administration coming in. I don't know at this point.

Even though the process was not integrated, this participant was hopeful for future administration to make that step.

As you know, leadership is not there yet. It has to come from the top, and it is not there yet. But, as we move forward, those links between outcomes, strategic planning and budgeting will happen. It just so happens [that] last year, when we start our budget in September/October for the following year, and because we had to get the budget done, we had to back into the linkages.

One respondent did not feel a link was necessary because they do not have budget constraints; however, the participant alluded to a strategic roadmap not linked to budget.

There is no link and that has never been an issue with us. Money has never been a constraint with the evolution of the business school. So, again, the plan does not have that kind of precision; overall, it is just a roadmap really; we have not linked it to budget.

Summary of Section IV: Budget Integration & Resource Allocation

A major area of limited integration found in literature and in this study was the budgeting process and the allocation of resources as a component of the strategic plan. In this consumer-driven environment, students care little about the distinctions that sometimes preoccupy the academic establishment . . . instead, they care about results (Spellings, 2006). Higher education institutions can no longer operate with internal silos; they must direct movement toward concepts of efficiency and accountability. Higher education has a duty of accountability to the public, governmental and private sources of funding; academic leaders must rise to the challenge of the new century.

There continues to be challenges to integrate outcomes assessment and budget; the budget and outcomes assessment are often viewed as separate entities apart from the strategic plan.

Participants specifically focused on the limitations in budget and the allocation of funds across all academic units. In addition, they expressed concern about the linkage of budgets to student learning outcomes assessment. The requirement of funds in the academic programs was another factor. Only one participant felt strongly about the strategic plan driving the budget and not the opposite and stated, "Strategic plans must drive the budget. To set it up any other way is silly, and it is a recipe for mediocrity."

CHAPTER 6
RESULTS OF RESEARCH QUESTIONS

The purpose of this qualitative study was to reveal the perspectives of higher education business unit leaders on the creation and implementation of a strategic plan. The perspectives of higher education business unit leaders were obtained to create a picture of reality for the creation and 'implementation of strategic plans. These participants have been exposed, in either their educational or experiential background, to the models and practices of strategic planning. They had the skills and expertise to pull together effective strategic plans for their units with integration into the institutional plan.

Creswell, 1994 stated, "Research questions are used as signposts for explaining the purpose of the study and guiding the research" (p. 78). The results of the data analysis provided rationale answers to the following research questions.

Research Question 1: How has the business leaders' education prepared them for strategic planning?

One hundred percent of the participants responded, with varying levels of confidence gained either from education, experience, or both, that they were competent to be leaders in business units in their colleges/universities. Participants stated that their continued work towards good strategic planning within their business departments would help in the integration of strategic planning within the institution. Several participants perceived that they had an advantage over their colleagues in understanding and implementation of strategic plans. Some mentored others in their institutions.

Research Question 2: What drives the need for strategic planning in the institution and business units?

Higher education business unit leaders in this study identified (a) executive administration direction and (b) the mission of the institution as major internal driving forces. The external drivers for strategic planning, in contrast to the literature, were (a) market penetration and (b) competition to remain a viable institution. The unit specialty accreditation, like IACBE, played a motivational role in the participants' strategic plan creations. Participants perceived minimal motivation from the regional accrediting bodies. Consistent with this phenomenon was the lack of transparency to the academic community; participants perceived that both internal publication and participation and external information were not divulged.

Research Question 3: How are strategic plans implemented in business unit programs and integrated within their colleges/universities?

The participants indicated that no facilitator was necessary for the creation of their strategic plans. Budget constraints and lack of institutional knowledge were common reasons why they did not choose to have facilitators.

The structural approach used in the institutional strategic planning process played a major role in the perspectives of the business unit leaders. Integrating the business units' strategic plans with the organizations' strategic plans was challenging, in either a bottom-up or top-down approach. Integration required a clear understanding of the organization's mission and goals. Both structures (i.e., top-down and bottom-up) showed a lack of integration with the creation of strategic plans by other departments in the institution. In addition, budget allocation and assessments were found to be limitations of both top-down and bottom-up approaches.

Research Question 4: How are their strategic plans created?

External market information surfaced as the greatest driving force for strategic planning. None the less, only an internal SWOT analysis, with minimal external factors, was completed in both top-down and bottom-up structural approaches. Participants agreed that setting goals and objectives drove their plans, but most found it difficult to create clear objectives and complete action plans.

The basic framework used was closely related to the literature's top-down model. Participants perceived the framework to be defined by a simplified list of seven *essential elements* important in the creation of strategic plans. Participants perceived the *top-down process* to be driven by executive administration.

1. Mission & Institutional Goals
2. Environmental Scanning
   a. SWOT analysis
   b. Market analysis (shown need, rarely completed)
   c. Student Learning Outcomes Data
3. Strategy Formulation
   a. Goals (some units are linked to institutional goals)
   b. Objectives: student learning and operational
4. Implementation - Action plans
5. Assessment – measurement tools

6. Budget Integration

The process perceived in the *bottom-up structure* was similar and was governed by the participants and perhaps by other unit leaders in the institutions.

1. Mission and Goals of the Institution
2. Environmental scanning
   a. SWOT analysis - isolated to the business units with little input from outside stakeholders, difficulty to get buy-in from faculty.
   b. No market analysis.
   c. Student learning outcomes data.
3. Strategy formulation
   a. Lack of focus from administration
   b. Frustration in setting goals and objectives
   c. The participants responded that even though the personnel in their departments were asked to participate in this annual process, there was very little buy-in.
4. Action plans and budget requests sent to the Provost/VPAA for integration.
5. All participants reviewed their strategic plans at least annually but rarely reported their progress.

Strategic planning was completed on an annual basis by 10 of the participants, nine completed a 3-5 year plan, and one had a two-year plan. All participants reviewed their strategic plans at least annually; the majority followed an academic calendar, rather than an annual or fiscal year calendar. The participants reported that even though the personnel in their departments were asked to participate in this annual process, there was very little buy-in; they perceived this factor to be a challenge to effective strategic planning.

Successful strategic plans were assessed with two frequently used tools: student learning outcomes assessment and operational objectives assessment. Participants expressed a disconnect with integration of outcomes assessment measurement and the overall strategic plan. Some student learning outcomes plans were separately created within units and were not connected to strategic planning.

Operational objectives assessment included the following measurement tools: enrollments; retention; graduation rates; resource allocation; and surveys directed to alumni, student satisfaction, and employers of graduates.

Research Question 5: What are the constraints/limitations of the strategic planning process?

The limitations and the enhancement can be found in each of the sections or themes. The primary limitation was the lack of integration of a unit's strategic plan within the institution. The essential elements, according to the participants, needed to be simple, quantifiable and easily interpreted. Accumulation of data and lengthy analysis were probably endangerments to the completion or appropriate focus of plans. The constraints included (a) providing education about the planning process, (b) involving members of the business units, and (c) promoting buy-ins from members of business units. Participants speculated that (a) a clear focus of goals by institutional administration and (b) adequate financial resources would assist with development of an effective unit plan. Units relying on the top-down model reflected the factors and sequence described in Figure 2; Units relying on the bottom-up model, however, reflected, with a significant number of limitations, the model described in Figure 3.

Research Question 6: What changes in the unit leaders' current process might produce a more successful product?

Changes identified by participants mirrored the limitations they described. The major enhancements included: (a) the integration of the created strategic plans into the overall institutional plan to ensure fair allocation of financial resources, (b) the involvement and buy-in from members of business units, and (c) continued education of faculty to the process of strategic planning and, (d) the simplification and accumulation of data coupled with sufficient time to analyze and complete the plan.

CHAPTER 7
GROUNDED THEORY

A **theory**, in the general sense of the word, is the analysis of data or observations with relationships to one another. Two characteristics of theory design are the constant comparison of data with emergent themes and categories to maximize similarities and differences of information (Creswell, 2009). Theory makes sense of the reality of the data and a given phenomena. This discovery "fits or works" in a substantive or formal area (though further testing, clarification, or reformulation is still necessary), since the theory has been derived from data, not deduced from logical assumption (Glaser & Strauss, 2008).

Grounded Theory & Model

The appropriate qualitative research method of grounded theory, (Glaser & Strauss, 1967; Strauss & Corbin, 1990; Glaser and Strauss, 2008;) was employed in this research. This methodology generates theory, particularly when studying an area in which the "relationships between concepts are poorly understood or conceptually undeveloped" (Strauss & Corbin, 1990). According to Byrne, (2001); grounded theory provides the researcher with strategies that can be used to build theories in areas previously unexplored or under explored.

Previous studies were predominantly quantitative; participants were surveyed to inquire about the use of strategic plan elements. The under explored area of strategic planning, using qualitative methods, revealed a more in-depth understanding and perspective of the participants. Specifically, the perspectives of middle management business unit leaders were sought and analyzed to learn about their creation and implementation of strategic plans. This evidence was presented in the grounded theory storyline in Chapter 5.

The themes emerged through analysis of the exploration of a "real world" grounded theory model based on participants' perspectives. The perspectives of collegiate business unit leaders addressed aspects of strategic planning creation. The emergent model addressed challenges and issues that leadership should consider in adapting the process.

With regard to strategic planning creation, the participants may have been confident in their knowledge of corporate strategic planning, but they expressed frustration in the application of those models to academia. In addition, the participants reported that the concept of strategic planning was underdeveloped for business units and, at times, for the institution.

In 50% of the institutions having business units, the executive leadership of the organization directed the strategic planning process in a top-down manner. The middle management leadership of the business units in these 10 institutions understood the directions of the institution and created the department's strategic plan based on the mission and goals of the institution.

The remaining 50% of the business units operated using a bottom-up process, and the focus of the strategic plan from the institutional leadership was weak. The participants linked unit goals to those of the institutions, but the business units' strategic plans were driven primarily by market competition and the specialty accreditation of the IACBE. In the remainder of this chapter, the researcher presents four theories that are grounded in data analysis.

Theory I: Driving Forces

The strongest driving forces for strategic planning, in order of influence, are (a) internal executive administration, (b) external market competition, and (c) specialty accreditation by IACBE in either a top-down or bottom-up process.

Without a driving force behind the creation of a unit's strategic plan, the institutions' executive administration served as the most important driver for the business unit's strategic plan and ultimate integration with the institutional plan. The need to stay viable as an institution and as a unit encouraged external market-driven planning for the majority of business units. The specialty accreditation of IACBE was the primary driving force for the business units. The regional accrediting bodies (e.g., Higher Learning Commission) had little impact on the creation of a unit's strategic plan. The researcher anticipates that when regional accrediting bodies have outcomes assessment in check for its members, the next focus of the regional accrediting bodies will be strategic planning with both student and operational assessment driving the plan as well as input to the budget. This analysis is evident in the literature requiring an institution to be more accountable and transparent to the public (Spellings, 2006) and is illustrated in Figure 6.

104

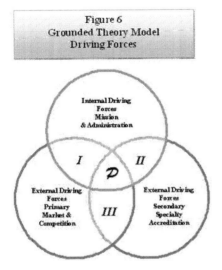

P In the center depicts the strategic plan with overlapping internal and external forces as motivation to the business leaders.
I: Depicts the need for administration to give attention to external market factors when creating a strategic plan
II : Recommendation of knowing accrediting body requirements when creating a strategic plan.
III : Understand the FULL environment when creating a strategic plan.

Figure 6. Grounded theory model driving forces

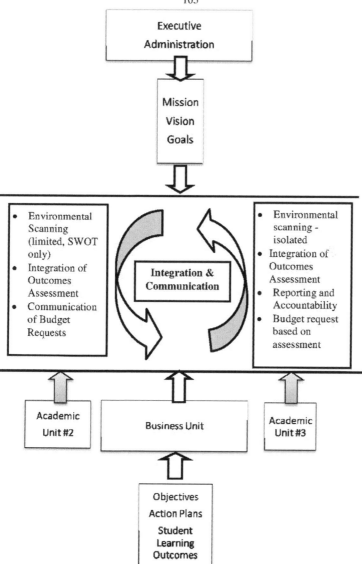

Figure 7. Grounded theory model strategic planning.

Theory II: Communication & Education

Communication and education of the strategic planning process must be clear for the business unit's personnel in a bottom-up process. This education is also required when the process is top-down where the business unit's strategic plan is integrated into the institution's strategic plan.

All participants reported that education of their business unit's personnel in their business unit's process and terminology of strategic planning was very important. When this was not done, the participants had difficulty getting buy-in from their faculty and staff. This is also true for the executive administration and the communication of the planning process for all constituents in the organization in a top-down process. Figure **7** illustrates the model that emerged from this study.

Integrating the business unit's strategic plans to the organization's strategic plan can be challenging either in a bottom-up or top-down approach. This required a clear understanding of the organization's mission and goals to be easily integrated. Both structures showed a lack of integration with creation of incomplete strategic plans by other departments in the institution. In addition, budget allocation and assessment were found to be limitations of both approaches.

Theory III: Assessment Integration

The basic framework for creation of the strategic plan was closely related to the literature models. The outcomes assessment of student learning and operational assessment were not used in all processes. This was revealed in the business unit's measurement tools and the integration into the institutional plan. There was also a lack of assessment data to drive the budget allocation.

The model includes the structural types of strategic planning, (1) top-down mission, vision and goals from administration and, (2) the bottom-up objectives, action plans, and student learning outcomes. However, both approaches show a lack of integration and communication as well as incomplete or lack of strategic plans in the other academic units.

More specifically, from the top-down executive administration, the gaps were found to be,

- Environmental Scanning (limited to SWOT only, no market analysis). Environmental scanning was limited to a SWOT strengths, weakness, opportunities, and threats analysis. A full market analysis was not completed for the majority of the institutions.
- Institutional communication of the process and use of assessment tools. Even though the mission, vision and goals of the institutions were followed by the business unit leaders,

there was a lack of outcomes assessment integration and understanding of business unit's and institutional planning processes and budget allocation.

In the bottom-up model, mirrored much of the same issues,

- Environmental Scanning (limited to SWOT in the business unit only, no market analysis) Environmental scanning was limited to a SWOT analysis within the business unit, with rare input from advisory boards and students input. A full market analysis was not completed any of the business units.

- If outcomes assessment were used, it did not drive the strategic plan but was a separate plan not integrated.

- Integration and accountability reporting of the business unit's strategic plan has been frustrating for these participants. Where the majority of participants in bottom-up processes do report to executive administration, they cannot be sure that their reports are read or used in the integration with other academic units. This is depicted in the model with dashed lined arrows which is the uncertainty of other units completing a strategic plan. In addition, communication of plan decisions and budget allocation was not communicated back down to the business units.

Theory IV: Assessment & Budget Allocation

The budget allocation is rarely driven by integration of student learning outcomes into the business unit's strategic planning. A major area of limited integration found in this study is the budgeting process and the allocation of resources as a component of the strategic plan. There continues to be a challenge with outcomes assessment and budget integration; many view them as a separate entity apart from the strategic plan. To better integrate the student learning outcomes and operational outcomes to the budget the researcher believes that direct correlation should be made to all budgetary requests based on these assessments. In addition, communication of the budget allocation should be communicated to the business units as well as all other academic units used for development of action plans in the academic unit.

The bottom-up model has integration challenges as well, these include: (a) environmental scanning isolated to the business unit, no market analysis, (b) integration of outcomes assessments to the business unit's plan, (c) Accountability reporting to administration, and (d) budget requests based on assessment.

CHAPTER 8
RECOMMENDATIONS

These recommendations are based on the perspectives offered by the 20 participants in middle management business units, the review of the current literature, and the experiences of the researcher. The following recommendations are provide by the researcher.

1. Business unit leaders, unsure of the strategic planning process used in institutions, should initiate discussions with the Provost/VPAA and President to clarify the process used. Inquire how the business unit (or other academic unit) fits into this process. The business unit leader should clarify:

    o How the business unit's strategic plan is to be incorporated into the institutional plan;

    o The expectation of budget allocation based on student learning outcomes;

    o The possibility of creating a process to integrate outcomes;

    o Reporting and accountability expectations of the business unit; and

    o The degree to which all departments are required to use the same process.

2. Business unit leaders should consider forming an advisory board of stakeholders that might include students. Such a panel could initiate and monitor annual environmental scans, using surveys, focus groups and demographics of the students.

3. Business unit leaders should invest time in educating faculty and staff about strategic plan creation to solicit and encourage "buy-in." Education includes knowledge of the roles in the process and accountability of action plans by periodic review of accomplishments.

4. Business unit leaders should provide information of how and why a unit plan is integrated into the institutional plan.

5. Business unit leaders should emphasize the importance of student learning outcomes and operational outcomes in the creation of a unit's strategic plan as a measurement tool for success and requests for budget allocation to the unit.

Implications for Practice

Accreditation, both regionally and specialty, will continue to drive the requirements for strategic plans in the future. The colleges and universities can use the personnel in the business programs to help with the process of strategic plan creation, gathering data and training for successful implementation.

A higher education integrated strategic planning model is needed and should be followed by the business unit and other academic units of the institution. Administration must drive this process and require accountability from all members of the institution with approval from the board of directors. This model should include measurement of both student learning and operational outcomes measurements to allocate scarce resources, and know where to place grant and foundational monies based on these outcomes.

This grounded theory and model has direct implications in both the business unit's strategic plan as well as the integration into the institutional strategic plan. In this study, the researcher has identified several factors that help to shape a model for business leaders to follow. Furthermore, the model shows gaps in the process that can be address in conjunction with the unit's leaders and executive administration. This communication can help shape the understanding and immediate importance of planning, not only form a market driven perspective, also accountability and transparency initiatives.

Implications for Research

The possibilities for further research on this new theory include:

1. Further research would be required to test this theory as the gaps are bridged in the strategic planning process.

2. Conduct a similar qualitative study with other types of institutions, i.e. public institutions and larger institutions, to obtain their perspectives of this model. This may lend additional depth to this model.

3. Engage other specialty accrediting bodies, like IACBE, to research similarities to this model.

4. Perspectives of executive administration Provost, VPAA and President's perspectives would add to the structure of this model. Their perspectives may change the grounded theories and model.

References

Accreditation Philosophy. (2006). Retrieved September 9, 2007, from International Assembly for Collegiate Business Education Web site: http://www.iacbe.org

Bann, C. M., Berkman, N. D., & Kuo, T. M. (2004, November). Insurance knowledge and decision-making practices among Medicare beneficiaries and their caregivers. *Medical Care, 42*(11), 1091-1099.

Basham, V., & Lunenburg, F. C. (1989). Strategic planning, student achievement and school district financial and demographic factors. *Planning and Changing, 20*, 158-171.

Birnbaum, R. (2000). *Management fads in higher education: Where they come from, what they do, why they fail.* San Francisco, CA: Jossey-Bass.

Bryson, J. (1995). *Strategic planining for public and nonprofit organizations: A guide to strengthening and sustaining organizational achievement.* New York, NY: Jossey-Bass.

Borgatti, S. (1997). Introduction to grounded theory. Discussion drawn from Glaser and Strauss. 1967, *The Discovery of Grounded Theory* and Strauss and Corbin,1990. *Basics of Qualitative Research* site: Retrieved October, 2008 from http://www.analytictech.com/mb870/introtoGT.htm

Bryson, J. M., & Alston, F. K. (1996). *Creating and implementing your strategic plan.* San Francisco, CA: Jossey-Bass.

Byrne, M. (2001). Grounded theory as a qualitative research methodology. *Association of Perioperative Registered Nurses, 73*(6). Retrieved September 12, 2002 from http://www.aorn.org/journal/2001/junerc.htm

Chermack, T. J. (2003). A methodology for assessing performance-based scenario planning. *Journal of Leadership and Organizational Studies, 10*(2), 55-64.

Chermack, T. J., Lynham, S. A., & van der Merwe, L. (2006, February). *Exploring the relationship between scenario planning and perceptions of learning organization characteristics.* Report presented by an Online Submission, Paper presented at the Academy of Human Resource Development International Conference (AHRD), Columbus, OH.

Cloud, M. (n.d.). *Strategic planning: An imperative procedure for educational leaders to employ .* Retrieved November 4, 2006, from ERIC database (ED 493 871).

Conrad, C. F. (1982). Grounded theory: An alternative approach to research in higher education. *Review of Higher Education, 5*(4), 259-269.

Cordeiro, W. P., & Vaidya, A. (2002). Lessons learned from strategic planning. *Planning for Higher Education, 30*(4), 24-31.

Creswell, J. W. (1994). *Research design: Qualitative & quantitative approaches.* Newbury Park, CA: Sage.

Creswell, J. W. (1998). Professionals' views of the "dangers" of self-help groups. In *Center for Research on Social Organizations(CRSO)* (p. 345). Ann Arbor, MI.

Creswell, J.W. (2009). *Research design: Qualitative, quantitative, and mixed methods approaches,* (3rd ed). Newbury Park, CA: Sage.

Cutright, M. (1997). Can chaos theory improve planning? *In The Best of Planning for Higher Education: An Anthology of Articles from the Premier Journal in Higher Education Planning.* Retrieved August, 2007, from ERIC database (ED 472 314).

Cutright, W. M. (1999). *A chaos-theory metaphor for strategic planning in higher education: an exploratory study.* Unpublished doctoral dissertation, University of Tennessee at Knoxville, Knoxville, TN. (ERIC Document Reproduction Service No. ED457931) Retrieved September 9, 2007, from ERIC database.

Cyert, R. M., & March, J. G. (1963). *A behavioral theory of the firm.* NJ: Prentice-Hall.

David, F. R. (2007). *Strategic management: Concepts and cases* (11th ed.). Upper Saddle River, NJ: Pearson-Prentice Hall. (Original work published 1999)

Denzin, N.K., & Lincoln, Y. S. (2005). *The handbook of qualitative research* (3rd ed.). Thousand Oaks, CA: Sage

Dirsmith, M., & Covaleski, M. A. (1983). Strategy, external communication and environmental context. *Strategic Management Journal, 4,* pp. 137-149.

Dolence, M. G. (Ed.). (2004). *Educause Center for applied research, research bulletin (10).*

Dooris, M. J. (2003). Two decades of strategic planning: Is strategic planning a useful tool or a counterproductive management fad? *Planning for Higher Education, 31*(2), 27.

Drucker, P.F., (2003). *The essential Drucker : The best of sixty years of Peter Drucker's essential writings on management.* New York, NY: HarperCollins

Eaton, D. R. (1989). *Strategic thinking about institutional direction.* Unpublished doctoral dissertation, Nova University, Online. Retrieved September 7, 2007, from ERIC database (ED318319).

Fâyol, H. (1975). *The principles and practice of management.* London; New York : Longman.

Ferrell, O., Hartline, M., Lucas, G., Luck, D. (1998). *Marketing strategy.* Orlando, FL: Dryden Press.

Ford, M. W. (2000). [Review of the quarterly quality report *Conceptual Foundations of Strategic Planning in the Malcolm Baldrige Criteria for Performance Excellence*]. *ASQ Quarterly Quality Report, 7*(1). Retrieved January, 2000, from American Society of Quality Web site: http://www.asq.org////_issue1/.html

Foster, W. (1990, April). The administrator as a transformative intellectual. *Peabody Journal of Education, 66*(3), 5-18.

Glaser, B. (1978). *Theoretical sensitivity*. Mill Valley, CA: Sociology Press.

Glaser, B. G., & Strauss, A. L. (1967). *The discovery of grounded theory*. New York, NY: Aldine de Gruyter.

Glaser, B. G., & Strauss, A. L. (2008). *The discovery of grounded theory: Strategies for qualitative research*. New Brunswick, NY: AldineTransaction.

Goncalves, K. (1997). Those persons who do your planning. In *The Best of Planning for Higher Education: An Anthology of Articles from the Premier Journal in Higher Education Planning*. (Reprinted from *Journal in Higher Education Planning*, 1997, pp. 303-307). Retrieved Spring, 2007, from ERIC database (ED472314).

Goodstein, L., Nolan, T., & Pfeiffer, W. (1993). *Applied strategic planning: A comprehensive guide*. New York: McGraw-Hill.

Hache, D. (n.d.). *Strategic planning of distance education in the age of teleinformatics*. Retrieved September 9, 2007, from Ontario Institute for Studies in Education of the University of Toronto Web site: http://www.westga.edu/~distance/.html

Hambright, G., & Diamantes, T. (2004a). *An analysis of prevailing K-12 educational strategic planning models* . Retrieved from EBSCO database (AN15068479).

Hambright, G., & Diamantes, T. (2004b). Definitions, benefits, and barriers of K-12 educational strategic planning. *Journal of Instructional Psychology, 31*(3), 223-228.

Handbook of accreditation standards. (n.d.). Retrieved September 9, 2007, from The Higher Learning Commission Web site: http://www.ncahlc.org

Hatch, J. (2002). *Doing qualitative research in educational settings*. New York: State University of New York Press.

Hill, T. (1997). Manufacturing strategy - keeping it relevant by addressing the needs of the market. *Manufacturing Systems, 8*(5), 257-64.

Hitt, M. A., Ireland, R. D., & Hoskisson, R. E. (2007). *Strategic management: Competitiveness and globalization*. Mason, OH: Thomson South-Western.

IACBE: International Assembly for Collegiate Business Education, Statement of purpose, (2006), www.iacbe.org.

Janaro, R. E., & Bommer, M. R. (2005). An integrative planning model for college and university programs. *Planning for Higher Education, 33*(2), 5-14.

Jones, L. W. (1990). Strategic planning: The unrealized potential of the 1980s and the promise of the 1990s. *New Directions for Higher Education, 70*, pp. 51-57.

Kaplan, R. S., & Norton, D. P. (1996). *Translating strategy into action: The balanced score card*. Boston, MA: Harvard Business School Press.

Keller, G. (1988). *Academic Strategy: The management revolution in American higher education*. Baltimore, MD: Johns Hopkins University Press. (Original work published 1983).

Keller, G. (1993). Strategic planning and management in a competitive environment. *New Directions for Institutional Research, 77*, 9-16.

Keller, G. (1997). The best of planning for higher education: An anthology of articles from the premier journal in higher education planning [Special section]. *Society for College and University Planning*, 1-335. Retrieved September 10, 2007, from ERIC database: http://www.eric.ed.gov///sql/_storage_01/////.pdf

Keller, G. (1999-2000). The emerging third stage in higher education plannin. *Planning for Higher Education, 28*(2), 1-7.

Kezar, A. (2005). Consequences of radical change in governance: A grounded theory approach. *The Journal of Higher Education, 76*(6), 635-667.

Kotter, J. P. (1995). Leading change: Why transformation efforts fail. *Harvard Business Review, 73*, 59-67.

Leonard, D., & McAdam, R. (2001, December). The relationship between total quality management (TQM) and corporate strategy: The strategic impact of TQM. *Strategic Change, 10*, 439-448.

Lincoln, Y.S., Guba, E.G. (1998). *Naturalistic inquiry*. Beverly Hills, CA: Sage.

Luu, H. N. Q. (2006). *Strategic plans in higher education: Planning to survive and prosper in the new economy* (Version ERIC Database) [Data file]. Retrieved September/30, 2006, from ERIC database (ED493377).

Martin, J. L. (1993). *Academic deans: An analysis of effective academic leadership at research universities.* Paper presented at Annual Meeting of the American Educational Research Association , Atlanta, GA.

Maxwell, J.A., (1996). *Qualitative research design: An interactive approach.* Thousand Oaks, CA: Sage.

McLaughlin, G., McLaughlin, J., & Kennedy-Phillips, L. (2005). Developing institutional indicators: The role of institutional research. In *Annual Forum of the Association for Institutional Research (AIR)* . Chicago, IL: DePaul University. Retrieved September 8, 2007, from ERIC database (ED491029).

Merrium, S. (1998). *Case study research in deduction: A qualitative approach.* San Francisco, CA: Jossey-Bass.

Miles, M.B., Huberman, A.M. (1994). *Qualitative data analysis* (2nd ed), Thousand Oaks, CA: Sage.

Mintzberg, H. (1978). Patterns in strategic formation. *Management Science, 24*(9), 934-948.

Mintzberg, H. (1994). The fall and rise of strategic planning. *Harvard Business Journal, 1*(59), 107-114.

Minzberg, H. (1994). *The rise and fall of strategic planning; Reconceiving roles for planning, plans, planners.* New York, NY: The Free Press.

Morris, J.M. (2002). *Readme first: For a user's guide to qualitative methods.* Newbury Park, CA: Sage.

Pacios, A. R. (2004). Strategic plans and long-range plans: Is there a difference? *Library Management, 25*(6), 259-269.

Patton, M. Q. (1990). *Qualitative evaluation methods* Newbury Park, CA: Sage, (pp. 169-186).

Porter, M. E. (1985). *Competitive Strategy.* New York: Free Press. (Original work published 1980).

Potter, W. J. (1996). *An analysis of thinking and research about qualitative methods.* Mahwah, NJ: Lawrence Erlbaum.

Randolph, L. (2006). *Leadership through partnership: A collaborative, strengths-based approach to strategic planning.* Paper presented at Academy of Human Resource Development International Conference (AHRD), Columbus, OH. (February Symp. 51-2).

Rieger, B. J. (1994). Strategic planning in public schools. *Catalyst for Change, 23*, pp. 9-15.

Roller, R. H., Bovee, S. L., & Green, J. L. (2004). *Integrating strategic planning, budgeting, and outcomes assessment in Christian business education*. Presentation presented at Christian Business Faculty Association 2004 Annual April Conference, San Antonio, TX.

Ruben, B. et al. (2008). *Assessing the impact of the Spellings Commission: The message, the messenger, and the dynamics of change in higher education*. Washington, DC: National Association of College and University Business Officers (NACUBO).

Schein, P. R. (1985). *Organizational culture and leadership*. San Francisco, CA: Jossey-Bass.

Schwarz, M., & Nandhakumar, J. (2002, March). Conceptualizing the development of strategic ideas: A grounded theory analysis. *British Journal of Management, 13*(1). Retrieved September 11, 2007, from EBSCO database (10453172).

Seagren, A.T., Wheeler, D.W., Creswell, J.W., & Miller, M.T. (1994). *Academic leadership in community colleges*. Lincoln, NE: University of Nebraska Press.

Seidman, I.,(1998) *Interviewing as qualitative research: A guide for researchers in education and the social sciences,* (2nd ed.). New York: Teachers College Press.

Spencer, M. H., & Winn, B. A. (2004). Evaluating the success of strategic change against Kotter's eight steps. *Planning for Higher Education, 33*(2), 15-22.

Spelling, M. (2006). A test of leadership, charting the future of U.S. higher education. *A Report of the Commission Appointed by Secretary of Education Margaret Spellings*, Pre-Publication Copy September 2006, from: http://www.ed.gov/about/bdscomm/list/hiedfuture/reports/pre-pub-report.pdf

Spendolini, M. (1992). *The benchmarking book*. AMACOM.

Stralser, S. (n.d.). Benchmarking: The new tool. In G. Keller (Ed.), *The best of planning for higher education: An anthology of articles from the premier journal in higher education planning*. (Reprinted from *Planning for Higher Education*, 1997, pp. 308 - 312). Retrieved Spring, 2007, from ERIC database (ED472314).

Strauss, A., & Corbin, J. (1990). *Basics of qualitative research: Grounded theory procedures and techniques*. Newbury Park, CA: Sage.

Teal, C. R., Paterniti, D. A., Murphy, C. L., John, D. A., & Morgan, R. O. (2006). Medicare beneficiary knowledge: measurement implications from a qualitative study. *Health Care Financing Review, 27*(4), 13-23.

Watson, G. (1992). *The Benchmarking workbook: Adaptive best practices for performance improvement.* Cambridge, MA: Productivity Press.

Wheeler, D.W., Seagren, A.T., Becker, L.W., Kinley, E.R., Milnek, D.D., & Robson, K.J., (2008). *The academic chair's handbook.* San Francisco, CA: Jossey-Bass.

Yin, R.K., (2002). *Case study research: Design and methods (applied social research methods).* Thousand Oaks, CA: Sage.

34583935R00071

Made in the USA
Lexington, KY
11 August 2014